Elementary Teachers Guide (for children ages 6-8)
Corresponds to the first year of a 3 year cycle for Elementary.

TEACHER
Year 1

Published by:
Mesoamerica Region Discipleship Ministries
http://discipleship.mesoamericaregion.org/
www.SdmiResources.MesoamericaRegion.org

ISBN: 978-1-63580-074-6

Category: Christian Education

Translated from Spanish to English by:
Emily Gularte (Lessons 1-10, 46-52), Kindra Bible (11-30), Nancy Mong-Tocto (32-32), Barbara Santana (33-45)

Unless otherwise stated, all the Bible references are taken from the NIV version.

Contents

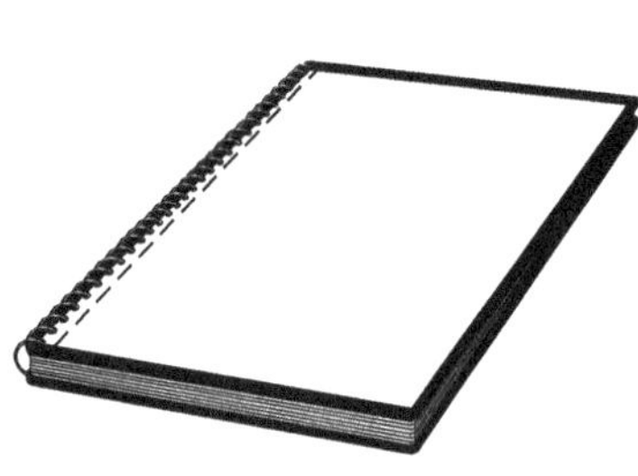

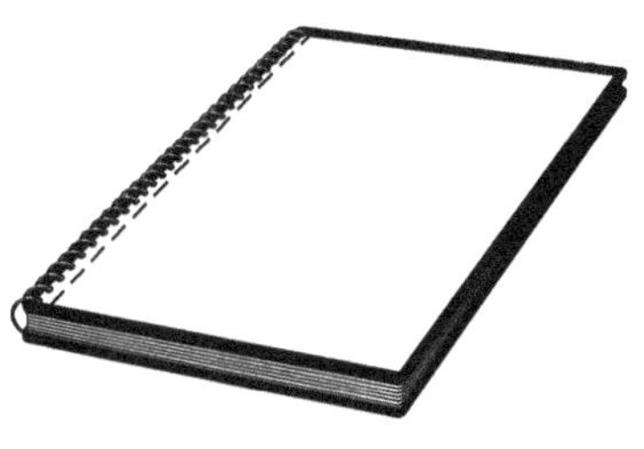

TEACHING RESOURCES

Dear Teacher:

We have prepared a series of teaching resources that will improve the dynamic of your class. Each lesson has an activities section, please use these materials to encourage your students to use their motor skills as well as help them gain a deeper understanding of the lesson. Prepare extra activities and crafts for the kids who visit your class.

LET'S MEET THE ELEMENTARY STUDENT

- ✘ They are active.
- ✘ They are excited about changes and new experiences, but they should not be over-stimulated.
- ✘ Their attention span is limited, especially with activities that require them to be still for a long time.
- ✘ In general, elementary students usually have 2 minutes of attention span for each year of age.
- ✘ They are inquisitive, so they will ask a lot of questions. Most often, they will ask "Why?" and "How?".
- ✘ They learn by doing, rather than by listening.
- ✘ Their learning is sensory, it is based on their senses, i.e. touch, taste, smell, see, hear.
- ✘ They do not have a long-term memories. Generally, they do not remember instructions for a prolonged period.
- ✘ They are selfish and egocentric, although they have begun to develop socially in respect to the rights of others, sharing, waiting their turn, etc.
- ✘ They work better in small groups.

In considering the characteristics of the development of your students, we have included these tips to help improve the dynamic of your class:

- ✘ Change the activity every 8 to 10 minutes. Alternate quiet activities with active games and provide a rest period.
- ✘ When a student asks a question, give them clear and truthful answers. Do not offer more information than has been requested.
- ✘ Involve your students in experiences that include direct use of the senses.
- ✘ Use repetition, both in telling the story and giving instructions.
- ✘ Use visual aids to stimulate your students senses, this will help them remember what they learn more easily.
- ✘ Organize games and activities that require everyone's involvement.
- ✘ Provide a quiet and unhurried environment.
- ✘ Remain calm when there is disorder and confusion.
- ✘ Give lots of specific examples of how to "share with others", "be compassionate", "be loving to others".
- ✘ Apply general ideas to specific actions in order to link Biblical truth to daily life.

RECIPES FOR PLAY DOUGH OR MOLDING CLAY

Flour and Salt Dough

Ingredients:

2 or 3 Cups of Flour
¾ Cup Fine Salt
½ Cup Warm Water
Food Coloring

Instructions:

Mix the flour with the salt and add the warm water little by little as you stir. If you want it to be colorful, add drops of food coloring as it thickens. The consistency of the dough will depend on the amount of water you add. Store in a closed container in the fridge.

Cooked Dough

Ingredients:
2 Cups of Flour
1Cup Salt
1 Tablespoon Vegetable Oil
2 Teaspoons
Food Coloring

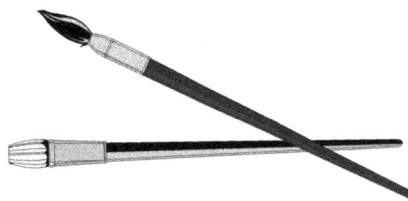

Instructions:
Mix the dry ingredients and then add the water and the vegetable oil. Cook the mix over low heat until it thickens, stirring it constantly. Take it away from the heat and let it cool. To make it the color you want, add drops of food coloring while you mix the dough. If kept in a closed container, it should last for over a month.

Mud Dough

Ingredients:
2 Cups of Dirt
2 Cups of Sand
½ Cup of Salt
Water

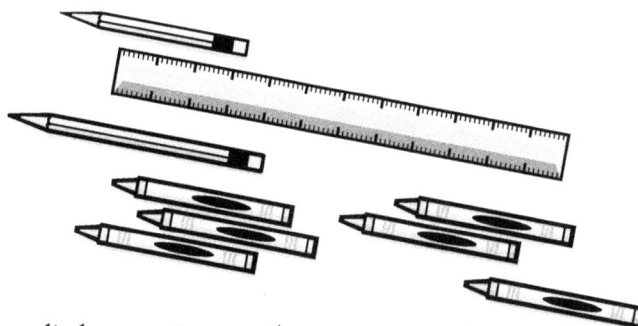

Instructions :
Mix the dirt, sand, and salt, and then add water a little at a time until you get a consistency that is good for molding.

Finger Paint

Ingredients:
1 ¼ Cup Corn Starch
½ Cup Powdered Soap
3 Cups Boiling Water
1 Tablespoon Glycerin
Food Coloring

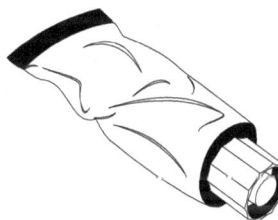

Instructions:
Dissolve the starch in cold water. Pour it into the warm water slowly as you stir to avoid clumps. Add the soap and the glycerin. To add color, use food coloring. This recipe is not toxic. If stored in plastic cups, it should last several days.

White Glue

Ingredients:
4 Cups Water
1 Cup Wheat Flour
½ Cup Sugar
½ Cup Vinegar

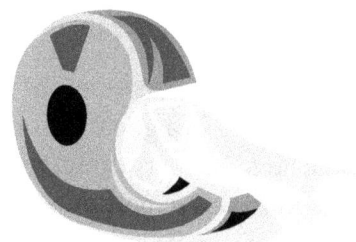

Instructions:
Boil 3 cups of water. Meanwhile, in a container, mix one cup of water, flour, sugar, and vinegar. When the water starts to boil, add the mix and stir slowly over the heat. If there are clumps, stir it more. If it is thick, add water. If it is too thin, boil it for longer. Store in a jar with a lid.

PAPER FOR CARDS AND CRAFTS

1. Soak 6 sheets of paper or pages from a magazine torn into small pieces in hot water.
2. Put it in the blender with half a cup of oatmeal or flowers or vegetables such as carrots or celery.
3. Strain the mixture and add 4 tablespoons of glycerin and 6 tablespoons white glue.
4. Spread the paste on a plastic sheet/tray with a rolling pin or stick until thin and even.
5. Let it dry in the sun for two days.
6. You can use this paper to make cards, bookmarks, letters, etc.

THE IMPORTANCE OF STUDENTS ADVANCING IN SUNDAY SCHOOL

Dear Leader and Sunday School Teacher;

As in elementary school, children in our church Sunday Schools should be able to be promoted to a higher level of Sunday School. As a classroom teacher, it is very important that you be prepared to promote the students at the end of the church year or, at the end of the school year - whichever is easiest. To accomplish this, talk to the Sunday School Superintendent of your church or your pastor.

You can prepare in advance a "ceremony" and give a certificate to each child passing to the next class. The ceremony can be performed in the sanctuary for all the congregation to participate in. Invite parents and relatives of the children. This will be a good time for them to get to know and attend the rest of the service and hear the Word of God.

It is important to have teachers of the classes that the children are graduating from and entering into as Special participants in the ceremony. It will be a special time for them to say good bye to their present teacher with a hug, and for the teacher of the next class to welcome them to their new class with a hug. At the ceremony, you can present a card decorated with photos of the children that have been taken during the year. It can include some memories of the child's participation while he was in class, Special prayers they said, the date in which they gave their testimony, questions that they asked, and moments of joy experienced in the class. Prepare the child in advance, so they are not surprised in front of the entire congregation.

Talk to the Sunday School Superintendent so that at the ceremony the new Sunday School book for the following year can be given to the student(s).You can encourage the families of the church to give a book to each child (as if they were the godparents), especially the children whose parents do not attend church or are at an economic disadvantage. In every congregation there are adults whose children are already adults who would gladly participate by giving a book to a child who attends Sunday School.

It is understandable if, because of a lack of teachers, it is not possible to have classes for every age group. This however is a good reason to invite and bring more children to church, and also to prepare and train new teachers. In every congregation there are always teenagers that are eager to learn how to teach a class. Do not miss this opportunity!

We wish you the richest blessings in the challenges that the ministry of education presents to you and your congregation.

In Christ and His Ministry,

Discipleship Ministries

____

(Child's Name)

Is Promoted to the Next Level Sunday School Class

(Church: *)*

Date

"My son, pay attention to what I say..." Proverbs 4: 20a

____

Sunday School Superintendent

____

Teacher

SUGGESTIONS FOR BIBLE MEMORIZATION

1. WHAT DOES THE VERSE SAY?

Have your students express what the verse says by using their senses.

See
In the Bible.
Visual Aids: on the chalk/white board, signs, posters, etc.

Hear
Read it out loud
Record it on a cassette and play it back

Speak
Repeat it after listening to it
Read it together and individually
Sing it

Touch
Write the verse.
Fill in the blank.
Solve a crossword
Use hand motions

2. WHAT DOES IT MEAN?

Explore the definitions.
Let the kids express what they understand about each Bible verse.
Explain words they don't understand.
Discuss the context.
For more explanation, use Bible commentaries, dictionaries and other resources.
Investigate the background of the verse.
Who is speaking and to whom are they speaking?
Discuss the facts.
Show pictures/illustrations of the text.
Create your own drawing.
Use hand motions, sign language or act it out.

3. HOW DO I APPLY IT TO MY LIFE?

Discuss the following:
- The daily life application of this verse.
- In which circumstances will it be useful and what effect will it have in your life and other's lives.

Remember a verse:
- When you are being tempted.
- When you are in trouble
- When you want to encourage others.

The Students, Their Behavior And The Teacher

1. Understand Your Students and Allow For Normal Behavior.

Children are active and curious.
They are not miniature adults: we must always differentiate between bad behavior and immaturity.

2. Create A Classroom Atmosphere That Leads To Good Behavior.

Let children know that you love them and appreciate them.
Show interest in what happens to them outside of class.
Be organized in how you handle the students.
Provide clear and consistent guidelines, let the children know what you expect of them.
Do not show favoritism.

3. Acknowledge Your Position As A Teacher.

Be in charge of the class.
Be a figure of authority that students can follow.
Become a friend to your students.
Explain to them what is expected of them and give them good examples.

4. Use Methods That Include Children and Capture Their Interest.

Be prepared and get to the classroom before any of the children.
Provide a variety of activities that are appropriate for your students' age.
Use activities that capture their interest and ability.
Allow children to choose some of the activities.

5. Focus on Positive Behavior.

Limit the number of rules.
When you correct a child, discuss it with their parent, guardian, or the person responsible for them.

WHAT DO YOU DO WHEN A CHILD MISBEHAVES?

1. Find the Cause of the Problem.

Does the child have learning or medical problems that prevent their participation in class?
Does he try to control the class?
Is he academically talented and therefore bored with the class?
When you know the cause of the problem, you may be able to correct it after talking with the child's parents.

2. Take Control of the Situation.

Ignore behavior that does not interrupt the class.
Include the child in learning activities.
Let him see that you are observing misconduct.
Approach the child in a loving manner.
Tell the child, quietly, what you want him to do.
Teach students the consequences of continued misconduct.

3. Talk to Parents or the Person Responsible for the Child.

If you know that you will most likely have to talk to his parents or guardian, do it.
Start by telling the parents what you appreciate about their child.
State the problem and ask for their ideas of how to resolve the problem.

Year 1 UNIT I

GOD'S PLANS FOR HIS PEOPLE

Biblical Basis: Exodus 2:1-15; 4:23; 13:17; 16:1-17; 19:1-20

Unit Theme Verse: *"Teach me to do your will, for you are my God..."* (Psalm 143:10a).

PURPOSE OF THIS UNIT

This unit will help your students:

✘ Seek God's direction.

✘ Feel reverence for the power of God

✘ Understand the care and patience that the Lord has for them.

✘ Learn to obey God in everything in order to live correctly.

UNIT LESSONS

Lesson 1: God's Plan for a Leader

Lesson 2: God Assigns Moses a Job

Lesson 3: God Rescues His People

Lesson 4: God Provides for His People

Lesson 5: Laws Given by God to Live Correctly

WHY WE NEED TO TEACH THIS UNIT

At this age, your students are discovering situations unknown to them previously; on occasion they will face a difficult problem and feel that God is not working in their lives. They may believe that being small means they can't do anything.

Through the lessons in this unit they will learn that we are all precious in the sight of God, regardless of age. They will also realize that the Lord is working in them NOW so they can learn from his Word while they are small.

They will learn that "obedience" and "availability" are needed to serve God; and God gives them grace and wisdom so they can obey and always be ready.

Availability is the desire to serve God. Moses is an example of a man who felt inadequate to the task to which God called him. At first he did not want to obey the command the Lord was giving him, to appear before Pharaoh and intercede for the freedom of his people.

However, God did not give up. Moses became a great leader who trusted fully in God, and through obedience, achieved true greatness. The Lord used him despite his lack of confidence and weakness.

Likewise, God can use children; no one is inefficient in God's hands, and children are no exception; they must feel that they are an important part of God's plan and know that they can depend on His help as they follow Him.

They will also learn that when they are in dangerous situations they can come to God with confidence, knowing that he is always willing to help them.

LESSON 1

GOD'S PLAN FOR A LEADER

GENERAL ASPECTS

Biblical Basis: Exodus 2:1-15

Memory Verse: *"Teach me to do your will, for you are my God..."* (Psalm 143:10a).

Lesson Objective: To help students recognize that God is always evident in the lives of his people.

TEACHER'S PREPARATION

The Hebrew people were enslaved by the Egyptians, because, after many years of enjoying their protection and sharing the land, a new Pharaoh had come to the throne. He was brave and arrogant and he didn't know Joseph, who had been a senior government official and saved the Egyptian people from starving.

Joseph's brothers and his father Jacob had come to live in the land of Gozen, where they settled and multiplied to be more than 600,000 people. The new Pharaoh was afraid because the Hebrew people were multiplying rapidly and there were more Hebrew people than Egyptian people, so he decided to make the Hebrews slaves because he was afraid that the Hebrews would try to take over his kingdom.

To remove this threat completely, he ordered every male child born of a Hebrew woman to be killed. However, God had great plans for the people of Israel, as He had promised to Abraham, Isaac and Jacob. He used a woman named Jochebed and Pharaoh's own daughter to carry out his plans.

Jochebed gave birth to a son whom she hid for three months. Then she took him to the river and put him in a basket to save him from death. Pharaoh's daughter, who was on the bank of the river, picked up the basket with the baby and decided to raise him as her own son. God used these people to carry out His plans.

Throughout all this history we realize how God reveals himself even in the most adverse situations, to fulfill his will.

(Present the lesson so that you students can see that just as God took care of Moses as a baby, He also cares for them and is evident in all aspects of their daily lives..)

ADAPTATION

Your students are starting to find themselves in situations unknown to them; And when they face circumstances that seem very complicated or difficult to accept, they may not feel that God is working in their lives.

Give a brief introduction to the Bible Story telling the students why the Hebrews lived in Egyptian. Here is an example:

"Abraham had a grandson named Joseph, who was sold by his brothers to be a slave in the land of Egypt. After many years, because Joseph obeyed God and helped save Egypt from famine, Joseph's family, the Hebrews or Israelites, went to live in Egypt because there was no food in the land of Canaan.

The Egyptians gladly received their new neighbors, and Pharaoh gave them the best land to live on and to work. However, many years later there was a new Egyptian Pharaoh who was not aware of what Joseph had done and did not want the Hebrews in his country. He thought the Hebrews were a threat to the peace of his people. "

Tell the story so that students understand the terrible situation God's people were going through, being subject to slavery and the death of all baby boys. Allow your students to participate by saying what dangers God saved Moses from while in the basket (drowning, starving, wild animals, etc..)

Talk about Moses childhood and imagine what his lifestyle in the Egyptian royal palace was like, and how this would differ from his Hebrew roots.

LESSON DEVELOPMENT

Introduction

Ask students what they know about Moses. Perhaps many remember the story of the baby inside the basket. Give some time for them to tell others what they know. If possible, give them paper and crayons to draw a picture of what they remember. This will help to illustrate the Bible story.

Read with students Exodus 2:1-15, and clarify anything that they may not understand before you start to tell the Bible story.

DEVELOPMENT OF THE BIBLE STORY

Gather your students to listen to the Bible story and prepare the material you deem necessary to illustrate the story in class. You can use a doll, drawings made by children or pictures that illustrate the content of the lesson. You will also need markers or crayons. Remember that the more dynamic the class, the more the story will impact the minds of your students.

The story of Moses is known to all. It is likely that the students have heard it more than once. However, remember that we can always find new and fresh ways to teach the Word of God.

APPLICATION TO DAILY LIFE

Establish a relationship between the Bible story and the lives of the students. Emphasize how important it is to know that God cares for us, because he loves us and has a special plan for our lives.

Ask your students, "What if your family had to be slaves to someone? How would you feel if you had to run away from someone who wants to hurt you? How would you feel if you had to live with a different family than your own?"

Let them answer and discuss their different views.

Emphasize that, despite everything bad that happened to Moses and his family, God did not forget them. Maybe they did not realize it at that moment, but God was carrying out his plan. He took care of Moses when he was just a baby because he would be a great leader who would deliver God's chosen people. Talk with your students about how bad things can happen to people who believe in God. Let them give examples (diseases, natural disasters, loneliness, poverty, wars, etc..)However, regardless of what might happen to us, we can always trust that God is working in our lives to carry out his plan.

ACTIVITIES

What Happens Next?

Using the worksheet from the student workbook that goes with this lesson, ask your students what is happening in each picture. Then cut out the four boxes with the pictures and glue them onto the correct sequence. When they have finished, review today's story using the worksheet.

The Funny Pencil

Ask the children to turn over the worksheet and follow the instructions to find the secret message. Read the words of each line out-loud. When everyone has found the hidden message ask all of them to read it together. The message is, "God has plans for you".

ADDITIONAL ACTIVITY

He is Always With Us!

Tell your students the following riddle:

"You can see what I do, because I am always at your side, moving the sails of a ship and the leaves of the trees, what am I?" (The wind)

When they have given the right answer ask, "How do we know that wind exists if we cannot see it?" Allow time for your students to discuss this point and come to a conclusion.

Give each of your students thin strips of paper, and ask them to go outside, hold one end of the strip with their fingertips and raise it up in the air. Ask, "What happens to the paper?" (The wind moves it.)

When they return to the classroom, sit in a circle and explain that, like the wind, God exists and we can feel him. He created everything that exists and He takes care of the world under his control. He uses people like Moses and like us to carry out his plans because He wants us to be part of his work.

We are God's special partners.

MEMORIZATION

Write the words of the memory verse on two sets of cards. Keeping the sets separate, mix up the cards. Divide the class into two groups. Allow the groups to come forward to put together the memory verse and to repeat it out loud together. The group to do it in the shortest amount of time is the winner.

Help them memorize the verse and ask them to go over it at home during the week.

CONCLUSION

Emphasize that today's story covers forty years of Moses' life, during which time, God was preparing him even though he was living in the midst of the Egyptians; and was unknowingly a participant in God's plan. We must also prepare to serve God in whatever he wants us to do (which includes going to school, obeying our parents and teachers, praying, reading the Bible, etc..)

Encourage students to trust in God no matter what.

LESSON 2

GOD ASSIGNS MOSES A JOB

GENERAL ASPECTS

Biblical Basis: Exodus 2:15; 4:23

Memory Verse: *"Teach me to do your will, for you are my God..."* (Psalm 143:10a).

Lesson Objective: To help students learn that God helps people accomplish the tasks he gives them.

TEACHER'S PREPARATION

When a Hebrew man asked Moses, "Who told you that you are our boss and can judge us?" (Exodus 2:14), he did not know how prophetic the words were! Prince Moses, the adoptive son of the daughter of the Egyptian Pharaoh was ready to be the boss and judge his people.

The land of Midian, where Moses had fled, was southeast of Mount Sinai, on the eastern coast of the Red Sea. It is believed that the Midianites derived their name from Midian, the fourth son of Abraham and Keturah. This town was dedicated to the care of sheep and the people lived in tents.

Moses married the daughter of the priest, Jethro, and worked as a shepherd looking over the sheep of his father-in-law. This work taught him how to survive in the desert where the Midianites had their home, and it was the way in which God was preparing him for the work that he would be entrusted to.

God himself revealed his plans using a burning bush to draw the attention of Moses. Fire is present in many of the revelations of God. It represents His holy presence. For the Hebrews and for many other nations of the past, fire was a special sign of a deity.

God wanted Moses to take his people out of Egypt. He said it would be a long process because Pharaoh would not let his slaves go; but God would always be with Moses, and would never leave him alone.

ADAPTATION

Like Moses, we often feel that God sends us difficult jobs to do. The same is true for your students; They find it hard to obey their parents when they are told to finish their chores instead of going to play with their friends; or return money they found, etc. These tasks seem so simple for us as adults, but involve so much commitment on the part of children, and they need to know that God is with them and helps them during all the difficult situations.

Our children are a part of a society full of sin. However, like Moses and like us, they are also called to help those who do not know Christ to be freed from the slavery of sin. It is important during the development of this lesson that they understand that when God asks us to perform difficult tasks, He also enables us to complete them and goes with us along the way.

LESSON DEVELOPMENT

Introduction

Write the following sentences on a piece of poster board or on the chalkboard:

(1) Please, God, send someone else to do the job!

(2) Please, God, send me!

Ask your class:

- ✘ Do you know someone who does not want to do what God has called them to do? (Let the children respond..)
- ✘ What do you think of those who do what they want regardless of the will of God?

Reflect on these two questions and say, "When God gives someone a job, the person can respond in two different ways." (Refer to the 2 phrases written on the board.) "What response do you believe the children of God must give?"

Encourage students to remember the stories of various Bible characters who decided to obey the will of God (Joseph, David, Joshua, Abraham, Peter, Jesus, John, etc..).

After the children have completed their participation, ask again, "What do you think would have happened if these Bible characters would have said to God: 'Please send someone else.'?"(Let them respond.)

DEVELOPMENT OF THE BIBLE STORY

If it is possible, illustrate your lesson with pictures related to the subject; as well as drawings, books or photographs about Egypt; have markers and colors ready for your students to use.

Show the pictures of Egypt to your students and let them study the pictures; tell them that the pyramids are one of the seven wonders of the ancient world, and that Egyptian civilization was remarkable developed for that time period. Show on a map of the location of the ancient Egyptian empire and its proximity to the land of the Hebrews. Briefly review the lesson from the previous class as an introduction to today's story.

Talk to your students about the living conditions of the Hebrew people when they were slaves, and emphasize what Moses did to defend a Hebrew.

Encourage students to imagine what feelings Moses was having leaving his family behind to go to an unknown place.

Tell how God revealed himself to Moses in the midst of a burning bush; and about the plans God had to free his people. Give the opportunity for students to participate and answer your questions as best as they can. It is important to understand God was preparing Moses, a long time beforehand, to help him lead God's chosen people.

APPLICATION TO DAILY LIFE

Very often children of this age may not feel able to complete some of the tasks entrusted to them, either at school, at home, or even at church. But they must know that when we seek God's will and we want to obey, it enables us to carry out what he commands us to do.

Moses was afraid to accept the work that God had given him because he did not feel prepared, but the very God who was calling him to serve would also enable him to complete the task.

ACTIVITIES

The Burning Bush

Give students the worksheet for this lesson and show them how to fold the paper on the dotted lines. Give them time to color the bush and put their name on the worksheet.

While the children work on their pictures, ask the following questions:

1. How would you feel if suddenly you saw a bush that was burning but not being consumed?
2. What did God ask Moses to do?
3. How did Moses respond?
4. What did God promise Moses He would do?

Emphasize that God gives us the help we need to do what he asks of us. He does not expect us to do it in our own strength. God promised Moses that he would be with him. In Exodus 4:12 God says, "Now go; I will help you speak and will teach you what to say".

The Funny Pencil

Explain to the children the instructions on the worksheet and help them find the special message that God has for them. (The pictures are: House, Horse, Balloon, Music, Cat. The answers are: collaborators, be, him. You may want to explain what the word "collaborators" means.)

Tell you students, "If you wish, you can decorate the worksheet and tell the Bible story to your family and friends."

MEMORIZATION

Have the children turn in their Bibles to the memory verse (Psalm 143:10) and read it out loud. After repeating it several times (by row, groups, and individually) allow them to come forward one by one to recite it by memory. Help those who have difficulty to learn it and ask parents to assist their child during the week by going over it with them.

CONCLUSION

To end the class, ask your students questions to review the lesson they've learned. Guide children in prayer and, if they have prayer requests, give them time to tell the class about their request.

Invite them to attend class next week to learn more about God's plan for his people.

Evaluate the participation of students and try to improve the areas where you feel that there are problems, and ask parents of children to encourage them to review with their children during the week what they have learned in class.

NOTES:

LESSON 3

GOD RESCUES HIS PEOPLE

GENERAL ASPECTS

Biblical Basis: Exodus 13:17; 15

Memory Verse: *"Teach me to do your will, for you are my God..."* (Psalm 143:10a).

Lesson Objective: To help students recognize and trust in the power of God.

TEACHER'S PREPARATION

The story in Exodus of the Hebrew people is one with impressive demonstrations of God's power. He saved Moses when he was a baby, and called him through a burning bush to be the deliverer of his people who were in slavery.

Until then, the power of God had not been demonstrated through only one man, but now he was ready to show his greatness in the midst of the Egyptian idols.

However, the Hebrew people were fearful and did not trust their new leader. They had not witnessed the presence of God like Moses had. But the powerful Egyptian Pharaoh and his priests felt no fear from a shepherd.

God clearly demonstrated his amazing power through Moses when God turned Moses' staff into a snake. When the Egyptian magicians recreated that same miracle, God sent plague after plague upon the Egyptian empire.

Each plague represented a direct attack towards the Egyptian idols. For example, the plague of blood in the water opposed Hapi - the god of the Nile; the plague of darkness opposed Ra - the Egyptian sun god; the plague that struck the cattle opposed Apis - the bull-shaped god of the cattle of the Egyptians.

One by one, the true God revealed the falsehood of the Egyptian idols. He showed his supernatural power to free his enslaved people; just as he would use a cloud and a pillar of fire to protect them while they traveled through the desert. The overwhelming demonstration of the power of God who parted the Red Sea is one of the strongest events in the history of the Hebrew people. The references to this event are very common in Scripture. Peter, Paul and Stephen all talk about it when referring to the faith the people of Israel had in the one God who is alive and wonderful.

ADAPTATION

Today, our children are accustomed to hearing about "superpowers" and fantastic events; but you need to make them understand that the only one who has power to do supernatural works is God, because He is the creator and sustainer of all that exists.

They must be assured that we rely on a powerful God, able to deliver them from the most difficult test. The story of the people of God can help increase their trust in the Lord who cares for and protects them.

LESSON DEVELOPMENT

Introduction

Talk to your students about who they believe may have superpowers or can do something that nobody else can do. Allow everyone to participate and, if possible, have them describe the person they admire most.

If you can, bring to class magazine clippings or drawings of characters that children consider to be "awesome". Show the pictures to the group and ask them to tell you what is real and what is just fantasy.

When you are finished, if you see that many of the students are confused as to why these characters are fake, explain that many of them are a product of the imagination of someone else and they do not really exist because the only one who can do something supernatural is God. Try to do it tactfully and let them see that it is important to only trust God for miracles. Say, "Today we will talk about something very special. We will study the miracles God did to free his people from slavery."

DEVELOPMENT OF THE BIBLE STORY

While telling the Bible story use as many teaching resources as you can. If you have a few pictures available, use them, or you might want to draw your own pictures if you have time. Keep your Bible with you as you tell the story, and stress the importance of studying the

Word of God. You also need crayons, scissors and glue for the children to complete their worksheets.

Tell your students to imagine they are in Bible times, living among the chosen people of God, and describe the difficulties they would encounter as slaves in Egypt.

Tell about the extraordinary way in which God demonstrated his power before Pharaoh and his subjects, through the plagues and how he commanded that they be punished for their hardness of heart. Illustrate the plagues using pictures or drawings, and encourage students to imagine what would happen if they were attacked by similar plagues.

Emphasize the care that God had for his people to free them from the plagues. Ask them, "How do you think the Hebrew people felt when they were finally free?"

God kept his promise to free his captive people and used Moses for this purpose.

Connect this lesson with the previous lesson and remind them of the fact that God had prepared Moses to guide the Israelites out of Egypt and never left him alone. God demonstrated his power and went with the people throughout their journey in the desert.

APPLICATION TO DAILY LIFE

Ask the children what caught their attention from the story, and talk about the love and protection of God for his people. Remind them that God also cares for us and keeps us from afflictions.

Explain that God can do supernatural things because His power is immense. He created everything that exists: the plants, animals, people, etc. Therefore, as our creator we need to be obedient and do his will.

ACTIVITIES

Crossing the Red Sea

Help students to cut out the figures and explain what they need to do to complete their worksheets. Tell them that this is their reminder of the Bible story and to take it home and tell their parents about what they learned.

How is the Sea?

Show your students pictures, photographs or illustrations of the sea, and ask if any of them have gone to the beach. You can supplement it with information about marine animals and plants. Emphasize the idea that only God has the power to open the sea as He did in the Bible story you told.

MEMORIZATION

Write the verse on the board or on a poster board, leaving blank spaces for words, so that children can fill in the gaps and then read the memory verse.

Ask for volunteers to write the missing words and read the entire verse. Then invite the class to put it all together and remind them to go over it at home during the week.

CONCLUSION

Encourage students to finish all their work before going home. Remind them to tell their friends and family today's Bible story.

Before dismissing them, express your joy of having them in your class and make them feel appreciated, loved and that you are interested in each of them and their families.

Invite a volunteer to say a final prayer.

NOTES:

LESSON 4

GOD PROVIDES FOR HIS PEOPLE

GENERAL ASPECTS

Biblical Basis: Exodus 16:1-17

Memory Verse: *"Teach me to do your will, for you are my God..."* (Psalm 143:10a).

Lesson Objective: To help students understand the care and patience God has towards them.

TEACHER'S PREPARATION

The people of Israel were like little children who needed God to teach them a new lifestyle. During the time they lived in Egypt they had turned away from him and his commandments.

Soon the Israelites forgot about the miracles that God had done to free them, and they were constantly complaining about everything that happened to them. The Lord had sent many plagues to punish the Egyptians for their hardness of heart, he had opened the Red Sea to let the Israelites pass, and protected them with a pillar of fire by night and a cloud by day. He looked after them with great love and incredible patience.

However, they continued to complain and speak against Moses. They were hungry in the desert and longed for the food that they had had in Egypt. God heard them and sent them quail and bread called "Manna" from heaven to pick up each morning. Manna was the main food of the Israelites during the forty years of their journey to the promised land.

But that was not the only problem; they cried about the lack of water and their complaints were even stronger. Moses suffered because of allegations that he received from the people. However, God's love and infinite patience remained intact and he provided his people with sweet and fresh drinking water from a rock. He kept showing his love for the Israelites, like a mother does with her hungry and whiny child.

ADAPTATION

Your students often show impatience and restlessness when their needs or desires are not satisfied. Through this story they may understand that God meets the needs of his children because He loves us and cares for us.

Students will realize that even when we feel God working in our lives we become impatient and complain, questioning his great power. Help the children understand that they must learn to trust in the Lord Almighty and be grateful for each blessing they receive.

LESSON DEVELOPMENT

Introduction

"A Walk In The Wilderness"

Take your students for a walk around the church and return to the classroom; hand out some cookies, chips or candy, but do not give them anything to drink, which will cause them to become thirsty. To introduce the Bible story start talking about what happens when we feel very thirsty.

DEVELOPMENT OF THE BIBLE STORY

Ask students to imagine that they are in the desert on a very hot day, and are very thirsty and all they can think about is a huge glass of cold water. Suddenly, in the distance, they see trees, plants and grass. Ask them, "What does it mean if there is vegetation in such a hot, dry place? Of course there must be water!"

Ask how many of them are thirsty and give them a glass of water. Then talk about how they feel now that they're no longer thirsty. Tell them that God showed his love for his people because while they were complaining and cranky, he was taking care of them.

Ask how the Bible story relates to what the students felt when they were thirsty, so they can understand what the people of God went through in the heat of the desert. Show a video clip or have some books that contain information and pictures about the desert.

Explain that sometimes it is difficult to trust when we are in the midst of a situation that makes us suffer. However, we can be sure that God will never leave us nor forsake us.

He always meets our needs because He loves us and cares for us.

APPLICATION TO DAILY LIFE

Invite a church member who has gone through a trial (hunger, disease, etc.) to give their testimony to the class. Ask the children to listen carefully, and when your guest has finished, urge your students to trust in God and no longer doubt that he always has everything under control.

If any of your students are going through a time of difficulty and find it difficult to trust in God, pray with them and remind them of the importance of not doubting in the power of God that is at work in our lives.

ACTIVITIES

God Provides Water for His People

Give your students the worksheet from the student book and read them the instructions. Give them time to connect the dots, creating a waterfall. Then help them cut out the arm of Moses (from the CUTOUT Section of the student book) and attach it with a fastener, so that Moses can hit the stone with his staff.

While doing this activity ask these questions, as a reminder:

- ✘ Why did the people of Israel complain?
- ✘ How do you think God reacted when hearing all the complaints of his people?
- ✘ How did God show his love for his people, even if they did not trust him?

Lasting Love

Write on the chalkboard or on a piece of poster-board Psalm 136:1 and read it aloud, "Give Thanks to the Lord, for he is good, His love endures forever." Ask the children:

"When do you think the Israelites might have said this verse?" (When God gave them manna, quail and drinking water.)

"What does this verse say about God's love?" (That it lasts forever.)

"God's love is wonderful and we can feel it every day in our lives."

Encourage students to draw a picture about the ways in which God shows his love to them.

Give your students the worksheet that goes with this lesson and have them complete the 2nd page. Help them fill in the blanks to complete the Bible verse. When they are finished, say the verse together.

MEMORIZATION

Write the memory verse on the board (Psalm 143:10) and read it with your students. Then remove the first and last words and ask for a volunteer to say it. Then continue to remove words until the board is blank and your students can say the memory verse completely.

CONCLUSION

Form the habit of praying with their students every time you have class. This creates a strong link between the teacher and the students, because the children feel appreciated and loved. Ask for prayer requests and commit to praying for them during the week.

Encourage them to pray and read the Bible at home and memorize the verse and tell the Bible story to their parents and relatives.

NOTES:

LESSON 5

GOD'S LAWS FOR LIVING PROPERLY

GENERAL ASPECTS

Biblical Basis: Exodus 19:1-20

Memory Verse: *"Teach me to do your will, for you are my God..."* (Psalm 143:10a).

Lesson Objective: To help students want to obey God in everything in order to live righteously.

TEACHER'S PREPARATION

When God called Moses to lead the Israelites out of Egypt, he promised them they could go to Mount Sinai to worship Him (Exodus 3:12.)Three months after they left, they reached the foot of the mountain. This visit had two purposes. The first was so that the people could receive the law of God, which gave them instructions to live properly; and second was for the people to become a nation.

The valley was at the base of the mountain and it was a good place for the large group of Hebrews to establish their camp. There was plenty of grass for the sheep, land for tents and drinking water. This was the place that God had chosen to make a special covenant with his people.

There are two types of covenants: the first type of covenant is one in which the two sides are equal in responsibilities and privileges; each party may act independently of each other, as in business or political parties. In the second type of covenant the parties are not equal; there is one party that is more powerful than the other who guides the other party, for example, a king and his people.

This second type of covenant was what God planned to make with the people of Israel. He promised them a powerful nation and that he would always protect them. Freeing the Israelites from slavery in Egypt fulfilled the first part of that promise. In return, the people were to obey God completely and honor Him, they were to put their trust and faith in Him alone and obey His laws.

The Ten Commandments were the basis of this special covenant.

It is easier if young children learn to live properly while they are young than it is to try and fix bad habits that they may acquire as they get older during the course of their lifetime. That is why it is so important to work with these young minds, and ask for the guidance of the Holy Spirit to direct their hearts to Christ's feet.

ADAPTATION

Teaching your students to obey the commandments of God will develop a respect for God and respect for the rights of others. At the same time, a foundation will be laid down so that your students will be able to live happier lives in obedience to the will of the Lord.

The Ten Commandments are a guide to help us in our relationships with the Creator.

LESSON DEVELOPMENT

Introduction

For the development of this lesson write the Ten Commandments on a large poster-board or piece of cardboard. For the activity "Is it Right or Is it Wrong?" have two bags or boxes and some small cards, crayons, blank paper and a ball or other small object.

Before starting the Bible story, start a discussion with your students about what would happen if there were no laws to guide what people are to do and not do; for example: What if there were no road signs? What if there were no safety signs in schools and hospitals? What if there were no laws to govern a country? Allow some time for the class to participate in this discussion; then help your students come to a conclusion that emphasizes that all these laws help us to enjoy a simpler and safer life. God has also made laws to help his people to live properly. Ask your students to pay close attention during the Bible story.

DEVELOPMENT OF THE BIBLE STORY

Talk to your students about laws. Let them know that there are laws that govern the behavior of people everywhere. There are laws in the country where we live, at school, at work and even within our own families.

These laws are rules that help us coexist in a harmonious way and avoid many problems.

Mention that God gave his people very special laws when they were in the wilderness that we too must obey because we are a part of God's family.

Make a poster with the Ten Commandments written on it (Exodus 20:1-17); you may wish to decorate it to look like the stone tablets that God gave Moses.

Show it to the students and tell the Bible story. Take a break after each commandment and allow students to give examples of what that commandment means.

Emphasize that God chose to speak to Moses because he was an obedient servant and he had a lot of faith. These commands helped the people to live in harmony and obey the will of God.

APPLICATION TO DAILY LIFE

Today's lesson will help students to understand that obeying our parents, loving our classmates, doing homework and not telling lies are some ways to keep the commandments of God.

Help them understand that God loves us and wants us to have a happy and abundant life, and that He gives us laws that help us behave and that help avoid problems.

ACTIVITIES

I Want To Love And Obey God

Give students the worksheet and colored pencils or crayons. Ask them to draw two pictures of how they can obey God this week. When they have finished, help them cut the instruction strip off the bottom and punch out or cut out the black circles at the top. Then insert yarn or a ribbon in the holes, so they can hang it in a visible place in their home.

Remind them to color in a star each day that they do what they promised.

Can You Repeat This Verse?

To complete the back of the worksheet, help the students find the Bible verse using the code.

Encourage them to repeat it together and then individually.

"Is this Right? or Is this Wrong?"

Use empty boxes or bags and several note-cards or small pieces of paper, and write on them the following phrases:

- ✘ Swearing when I'm angry.
- ✘ Taking my friend's toy, because I like it.
- ✘ Not obeying my mom when she tells me to do something.
- ✘ Hitting my friends when they don't want to play the same game as me.
- ✘ Doing my homework without being reminded.
- ✘ Helping my family with housework.
- ✘ Crying when my friends don't do what I say.
- ✘ Lending my toys to my friends.
- ✘ Always saying "please" and "thank you".
- ✘ Telling lies so I don't get in trouble.
- ✘ Being grateful for what I have.
- ✘ Arriving home early when my mom asks me to.

You can make as many cards as you wish. In one of the boxes or bags write the word "Right" and another "Wrong." Place the cards upside down on a table and have students take turns reading them. After reading the sentence they must state whether it is "Right" or "Wrong" and place it in the appropriate box.

The Ten Commandments are for me

Give each student a sheet of paper and crayons. Give them some time to copy the Ten Commandments from their Bibles or the poster you made onto their paper.

They can decorate their Ten Commandments as they please and take it home to hang in their favorite place. Ask if they have a prayer request and pray for all the requests.

MEMORIZATION

Write the memory verse on a chalkboard and say it out loud with your students. Erase some of the words, and let the children say it again. Repeat this action until all the words are erased and the children can say it by memory.

Ask your students what they learned in class today; you can do this by playing this game: Throw a ball or other light object to one of them. When they catch the ball they get to tell the class something that they learned from today's story. Then, that child can throw the ball to another classmate, and so on until everyone has had a chance to participate.

CONCLUSION

It is very important that you do not forget to pray before you end the class. Your students need to have the opportunity to thank God for allowing them to be in class again today. Ask them if they have any prayer requests and pray for them.

YEAR 1 UNIT II

THE TEN COMMANDMENTS

Biblical Basis: Exodus 20:1-13; 32:1-34; 1 Samuel 17:12-20; Genesis 31:1-35; 20:13, 1517; 1 Kings 21:1-20.

Unit Theme Verse: *"Obey the Lord your God and follow his commands and decrees that I give you today."* (Deuteronomy 27:10).

PURPOSE OF THIS UNIT

This unit will help your students:

- ✘ Put God first in their lives.
- ✘ Understand why it is important to honor and obey their parents.
- ✘ Not to lie or deceive others.
- ✘ Not to have bad thoughts.
- ✘ Understand that God gave rules to his people to obey.
- ✘ Know that God gave us these rules to help us live a better life.
- ✘ Understand that God will forgive them when they disobey and he will help them be obedient to his rules.

UNIT LESSONS

Lesson 6: God is First

Lesson 7: Honor Your Parents

Lesson 8: Always Be Honest

Lesson 9: Respect the Rights of Others

WHY WE NEED TO TEACH THIS UNIT

The vast majority of your students have heard the Ten Commandments. Many of them may even know them by memory. However, we need to reinforce their learning about the Ten Commandments in order for them to understand why it is important to obey them and apply them to their daily lives.

Many modern civilizations reflect the influence of the Ten Commandments in their legislative systems. Some governments use the last six commandments as a basis for laws controlling human behavior.

It is important to remind students that God gave these commandments to help his people. They tell us what the Lord expects of our relationship with him and with others.

Your students will learn that some of the Bible characters were obedient and others were not. They will be taught that disobedience brings serious consequences.

During this unit, you can ask for the guidance of the Holy Spirit to give you an opportunity to present the plan of salvation to your students, and give the invitation to children who have not made the decision to accept Christ as their Savior.

LESSON 6

GOD IS FIRST

GENERAL ASPECTS

Biblical Basis: Exodus 20:1-11; 32:1-34

Memory Verse: *"Obey the Lord your God and follow his commands and decrees that I give you today"* (Deuteronomy 27:10).

Lesson Objective: To help students learn what it means to put God first in their lives.

TEACHER'S PREPARATION

The first four commandments (Exodus 20:1-11) instruct us on our relationship with God. When Moses presented the 10 Commandments that God had given him to Israel, it symbolized the beginning of the relationship of the Lord with his people through a series of standards that expressed what his will for his children would be. Exodus 32:1-34. The story of the golden calf shows how quickly the people forgot what God had done for them. These people are annoyed and distressed because their leader, Moses, was gone. The request that they made "Come, make us gods who will go before us" did not necessarily mean that the Israelites were rejecting God, they wanted something visible to represent him and give them confidence.

Moses, the pillar of fire and the cloud met this need; but the people had not seen Moses for forty days and thought he would never return. Aaron granted Israel's request and built a golden calf for the people to worship.

They also built an altar to the new god and they offered it sacrifices. The Israelites were very happy to have the golden calf to worship, proclaiming that it was who brought them out of Egypt.

God was very angry because of the sin of his people and asked Moses to leave so that he could destroy them, but Moses sought God's favor for the people. This moment in the history of the Israelite people is evidence of their lack of faith and commitment.

Tell your students that to put God first should be a priority in our lives and that, as Christians, our goal should be to please him with our actions and words.

ADAPTATION

Most of your students, especially those who have grown up in the church, know that one of the commandments is not to worship false gods. However, this commandment refers not only idols made by men, but also to other aspects of life.

LESSON DEVELOPMENT

Introduction

Welcome your students and make them feel appreciated. Ask, "Who likes to travel or go for a walk?" Say, "I like that when I travel, whether in our town or to another town there are signs along the road that guide me. Can anyone tell me what signs I might see?"(Let the children participate and tell what signs they have seen, such as: stop signs, danger signs, use your seat belt signs, etc..)

Emphasize the idea that all these signs are rules that must be obeyed. Ask, "Why do you think these signs help us?" (Wait for their answers and explain that they help us to reach our destination, and warn us of possible dangers. If we obey them, we will have a good trip and be safe.) Mention that in the same way God has given us a set of rules that we call "commandments" and that they help us to live as he wants us to.

On a piece of cardboard or poster-board write the word "Commandment" in large letters and stick it up in your room. Tell students that during this unit they will learn about the commandments God gave to his people.

DEVELOPMENT OF THE BIBLE STORY

Before class time, look for drawings of a golden calf to show to the children.

Start the Bible story by describing to your students the situation that the people of Israel were going through. It had been many months since the Israelites had left Egypt; They had been walking in the desert for a long time and God had demonstrated many times that He was always protecting them. However, the people were continuously complaining and God had heard them.

Now they were at the foot of Mount Sinai. Moses climbed the mountain to receive the commandments God had for his people. After forty days, the Israelites thought Moses had died and they began to ask Aaron for a god.

If possible, show students illustrations of the golden calf and explain what the people did to worship the golden calf. Emphasize the fact that the Israelites were not giving God the place he deserved, and they had forgotten all the miracles they had seen since leaving Egypt.

Ask, "Can you imagine how God felt when he saw what his people were doing?"

"Do you think the people deserve God's forgiveness?" Give them time to answer and reflect on the importance of being thankful and loyal to God.

While you tell the Bible story, allow your students to see you are using your Bible. It is important that they understand that these teachings are found in the Word of God.

APPLICATION TO DAILY LIFE

Today our society encourages children to think of themselves first. Television programs and commercials urge them to do "what makes them feel good". Material possessions and pleasures occupy a more important place than God. People see the "Lord's Day" as any other day, and do the same activities every day. They do not understand the importance of keeping the Sabbath day holy.

Your students need to understand that there is a better way to live life and that better way is by following God's commands. Compare the disobedience of the Hebrew people to that of our society today and invite your students to put God first and obey his commandments.

ACTIVITIES

Write a Story

Give your students the worksheet from the student activity book. Read together the four commandments that are written there and ask,

"Which picture reminds you of the Bible story? Why was it wrong for the people of God to worship the golden calf?" Then give them some time to create stories about obeying and disobeying God.

Pictures and Vowels

Have them turn to the 2nd page of their worksheets, and give them time to complete the code, filling in the blanks that paraphrase the Bible verse, "Obey the Lord your God and follow his commands and decrees" (Deuteronomy 27:10).

Heart Puzzle

Prepare ahead of time several heart shaped puzzles. Write on each of them the phrase, "Love God With All Your Heart". Use different colors and cut them into five parts.

Mix up all of the pieces of the puzzles; then give one piece to each child (do not give five children in a row the same color, mix them up). Then tell them, "When I say 'Now!', you all need to find the other children who have the same color as you do and then put your puzzle together." Congratulate those who finish first and talk about the importance of loving God with our whole being.

MEMORIZATION

On note-cards or pieces of paper, write the words of the Bible memory verse (Deuteronomy 27:10) putting one word on each card. Then hide them around the classroom before the students arrive.

When the lesson is over, tell them that they will learn a new verse for this unit, but is lost. Have them look for the cards and bring them to the front. As they find the cards, put them in order on the board and repeat the Bible verse together. Use these cards throughout the unit as a tool for memorizing the verse.

CONCLUSION

Before dismissing the students, invite them to come again next week. Encourage them to put into practice, during the week, what they learned in class today. Hand out the worksheets they did and pray for them before they leave.

NOTES:

LESSON 7

HONOR YOUR PARENTS

GENERAL ASPECTS

Biblical Basis: Exodus 20:12; 1 Samuel 17:12-20; 22:1-4.

Memory Verse: *"Obey the Lord your God and follow his commands and decrees that I give you today"* (Deuteronomy 27:10).

Lesson Objective: That your students will learn why it is important to honor their parents.

TEACHER'S PREPARATION

The fifth commandment is the first commandment that deals with interpersonal relationships, especially family relationships. It shows the importance that God places on the family.

Normally we think this commandment is directed only to children, forgetting that it was given first to the Israelites who were mostly adults.

Adults also have an obligation to their parents to treat them with respect and honor. This is also the first commandment with a promise. God assures a long life to those who honor their parents.

1 Samuel 17:12-20 and 22:1-4. David is known as a shepherd who tended his father's sheep and killed the giant Goliath with a slingshot. Students have probably heard stories where David plays the harp to please the king. However, many are unaware of the story in which David takes care of his elderly parents.

When King Saul pursued David, he hid inside a cave. His parents had to leave home to be near their son during this time of difficulty. But he did not want to expose them to danger, so he took them to the region of Moab and asked the king to give them shelter. It is possible that Jesse, the father of David, had relatives living in Moab. The king accepted the request of David, and his family lived there for as long as David was in trouble.

ADAPTATION

It is important for your students to know about this part of the life of King David because it demonstrates the care and concern we should have for our parents. Children go through stages in which they have conflict with authority, usually parents or guardians.

They need to understand that obeying and loving their parents is not an option but a Commandment from God, a commandment that comes with a promise. Encourage students to recognize and value the importance of loving and honoring their parents throughout their lives.

LESSON DEVELOPMENT

Introduction

Have your students sit in a circle to hear the Bible story and then Ask, "Which of the commandments of God do you believe is easiest to break?" (Let them respond and write their opinions on the board or on a large sheet of paper.)

Then ask, "What happens when people do not obey the commandments of God?" After hearing their responses tell them that today they will learn how to obey the commandment that is the easiest to break.

DEVELOPMENT OF THE BIBLE STORY

Before class time, prepare the teaching resources you will need for this lesson. We suggest that if you have pictures that illustrate this Bible story, you use them; if you do not have illustration or picture, you can create/draw your own using cardboard or paper and markers or colored pencils. In one picture draw David as a shepherd; in another, David as a young warrior; in another, David as the king; and finally, David as a loving son.

Tell the story of David, showing the class the pictures and emphasizing that from the time he was small he helped his father with the household chores and as a shepherd to his father's sheep. Then, when he was in conflict with King Saul, he saw to it that nothing bad happened to his parents and took them to live in a safe place.

David wanted to obey God's command to honor his parents and worried about their safety. For this reason, the Lord fulfilled his promise to him and allowed him to live a long time and to reign for forty years as King of Israel.

APPLICATION TO DAILY LIFE

Once you have told the story, ask the students what they liked about it. Point out to them that even though David was a very important person and future king of Israel, he never forgot to obey God's commandments, including the commandment to honor his parents.

Encourage them to keep the commandments of the Lord by obeying their parents. Tell them if they have difficulties obeying than they can pray and ask God to help.

Allow time for everyone to tell their experiences regarding obedience to parents, and encourage them to be like King David, who cared and loved his parents even as an adult. Complete this time with prayer and intercession for your students.

EXTRA ACTIVITY

Fun Riddles

Read these riddles and allow the children to guess who the riddle is describing:

1. I sang a song that's in the Bible.
   - ✘ I helped my mother to save the life of my brother by putting him in a basket and taking him to the river.
   - ✘ I obeyed my mother by taking care of my little brother.
   - ✘ Who Am I? (Miriam, the sister of Moses.)
2. My parents were old when I was born.
   - ✘ I was the fulfillment of a promise God made to them.
   - ✘ My father sent a servant to find a wife for me.
   - ✘ My wife and I had twin sons.
   - ✘ Who Am I? (Isaac.)
3. I was the favorite son of my father.
   - ✘ He gave me a special coat that had many colors.
   - ✘ My brothers sold me as a slave and I suffered in a distant country.
   - ✘ I saved my family from starvation.
   - ✘ Who Am I? (Joseph.)
4. I am the youngest of eight children.
   - ✘ I took care of my father's flock of sheep and I played my harp to cheer up the king.
   - ✘ God helped me to kill a giant.
   - ✘ Who Am I? (David.)

ACTIVITIES

We Honor Our Parents

Give your students the worksheets from the student activity book, and help them cutout the pictures that go with this lesson from the CUTOUT section of the student book. Talk to them about which pictures show children honoring their parents.

Have them glue the pictures of children honoring their parents in the blank spaces next to the corresponding pictures on the worksheet.

Talk about the remaining pictures and ask, "What are these children doing that does not honor their parents?"

In the blank space located at the bottom of the worksheet allow your students to draw a picture of something they can do to honor their parents and discuss what they drew.

Then discuss the different ways in which children can honor their parents and make a list on the board.

The Labyrinth of Letters

Read the instructions and give some time for students to find the words hidden within the maze. When they have finished, read the sentences together.

MEMORIZATION

Have your students sit in a circle and give them a ball to be passed from person to person while you play music. (You can play a tambourine, ring a bell, play a CD, etc..) When the music ends, the child holding the ball in his hands must stand up and say the memory verse (Deuteronomy 27:10). Continue the game until everyone has had a turn to say the verse.

CONCLUSION

Give your students the work they did during class time and ask them to be sure and come next week. Say a prayer and be sure to include the requests of your students.

Evaluate the development of your class and look for ways to make the next class better, so that your students are continually learning something that is meaningful.

LESSON 8

ALWAYS BE HONEST

GENERAL ASPECTS

Biblical Basis: Genesis 31:1-35; Exodus 20:4, 15-16

Memory Verse: *"Obey the Lord your God and follow his commands and decrees that I give you today"* (Deuteronomy 27:10).

Lesson Objective: To help students understand why it is important not to lie and to always tell the truth.

TEACHER'S PREPARATION

Genesis 31:1-35. The story of Rachel and Leah is full of envy and jealousy. They were sisters, as well as wives to Jacob and daughters of the same father. They competed all the time and allowed Laban, their father, to treat Jacob unfairly.

One day, Jacob decided to leave the land of his father-in-law and go to Canaan, his hometown, and he took with him his wives, children, and livestock. Because of the resentment she felt toward her father, Rachel stole the idols that Laban had in his house. These idols were a common part of the religion of Mesopotamia and held special value to their owner.

Laban went looking for Jacob, and charged him with theft. Jacob did not know that Rachel had hidden the idols she had taken, so he gave permission for Laban to search through the camp, and he said whoever was found guilty of the theft would die.

Rachel was a smart woman, so she very carefully hid the idols in a camel's saddle, and sat on it. When her father came to where she was, she said she could not get up because she was not feeling well. She knew no one could force her to move. Rachel not only stole the idols, but she lied to hide what she stole and to protect herself.

We find no Biblical evidence that would reveal what happened after Rachel's deception. However, God was aware of the situation and knew her behavior.

The story today shows us how painful and how damaging it can be to relationships if we lie and steal. Jacob and his father-in-law were angry with each other, and Rachel and her children never saw Laban (their father and grandfather) again.

Exodus 20:4, and 15-16. The Ten Commandments explain the property rights of individuals; Theft is forbidden by the 8th commandment, "You shall not steal" (Exodus 20:15.)

Likewise, God condemns lying. The 9th commandment says, "You shall not give false testimony against your neighbor" (Exodus 20:16). Stealing and lying can damage relationships between people and more importantly our relationship with God.

ADAPTATION

Children at this age have many conflicts with lying, as it is a common practice in our society; the same applies to stealing. During this class it is necessary to emphasize the importance of guarding with love the laws of God that are contained in the Ten Commandments.

Remind your students that they should not rely on their own strength to follow God's rules. He wants to help us to obey Him and he forgives those who have done something wrong.

LESSON DEVELOPMENT

Introduction

Introduce the lesson by using a story that your students can participate in. Ask them to imagine they have a new bike, and one day after playing they forget to put it away. Ask, "How would you feel if someone had stolen your new bike?" Let children respond and say, "Now imagine that the next day you see one of your friends using your new bike and, when you ask them about it, they say that it was a gift from their parents. How would you feel now?"

Help your students understand that lying and stealing always hurts people.

DEVELOPMENT OF THE BIBLE STORY

Invite someone to represent Rachel and tell today's story. It is important to start from the moment that we meet Jacob until he flees to Canaan. It is important to emphasize the consequences that stealing and lying brought Rachel.

If possible, get an object that can represent the idols of Laban and a pillow to serve as a saddle and act out the part of the story where Rachel hides and sits on the idols. This way they can imagine the way that Rachel hid what she had stolen.

Allow time for your students to ask questions and also tell about their experiences with stealing and lying.

Read Exodus 20:1-17 and have students identify the commandments that today's lesson refers to.

APPLICATION TO DAILY LIFE

When people make a mistake they fear being discovered and punished. Not telling the truth or lying is a way to avoid the consequences of our actions. Other times, honesty and speaking the truth can mean having to face consequences that are not pleasant.

Likewise, when we are seeking acceptance among our friends we exaggerate reality or hide details of our life that seem unpleasant, which is also a lie.

Children need to understand that lying is a sin and it breaks one of the Ten Commandments.

Likewise stealing, or to not return something borrowed or hiding something that is not theirs is not pleasing to God, and sometimes they do not know this. Through this lesson emphasis to your students that these are sins that are regulated by the laws of God, which we must always obey.

ACTIVITIES

The Different Faces of the Robber

Have crayons and glue for the students to use to complete their worksheets.

Hand out the worksheets from the student books for this lesson and the relevant page from the CUTOUT section. Give them time to cut out the faces, and then talk about the different expressions Rachel had while she was stealing and lying. Provide them with glue and crayons to complete this activity.

Remind them that when we lie or steal we always hurt someone. God gave these rules to protect his people and to help them live in peace with others.

Would You Do That To Someone You Love?

You will find this activity on the 2nd page of the student worksheet. Read aloud the instructions and help your students complete the activity. Help your students draw conclusions from what they have learned in class and encourage them to think about how they can apply what they've learned to their daily lives.

Different Faces

Draw, using dotted lines, two incomplete faces on the board or on a poster. Make them large enough so that all the children can participate in completing them. One face should be happy and the other sad.

Read the following statements and ask for volunteers to determine if they are true or false. The child who answers correctly gets to complete a part of the face that corresponds to their answer (if true the smiling face, if false the sad face.) The next to answer can complete another part of a face and then the next an eyes the next the mouth, etc. Discuss why the face of truth is happy and the lying face is sad. If possible, write the phrases on slips of paper and let the children read them. You can add more if you want:

- ✘ I never get homework from school.
- ✘ Small lies are not really lies.
- ✘ God loves all people.
- ✘ An alien lives in my house.
- ✘ My mom never scolds me.
- ✘ Sometimes it's hard to tell the truth.
- ✘ I have a pet lion.
- ✘ We must love our neighbor as ourselves.
- ✘ The church is the house of God.
- ✘ We must always forgive.

MEMORIZATION

Provide paper and crayons for your students. Give them time to write the memory verse out and decorate it how they want to. When finished, allow your students to show their work to the class and say the verse out loud.

They can take their pictures home to put up where they can see it during the week and review their verse.

CONCLUSION

Before ending the class, clarify any doubts your students may have about the lesson and help them complete their work. Encourage them to practice the commandments they learned today throughout the week, and to tell today's Bible story to their friends and family.

Close with prayer and intercede for the specific needs of your students.

LESSON 9

RESPECT THE RIGHTS OF OTHERS

GENERAL ASPECTS

Biblical Basis: Exodus 20:13, 15-17; 1 Kings 21:1-20

Memory Verse: *"Obey the Lord your God and follow his commands and decrees that I give you today"* (Deuteronomy 27:10).

Lesson Objective: To help students understand that lying, stealing and murder start with bad thoughts.

TEACHER'S PREPARATION

Exodus 20:13, 15-17. The Ten Commandments are the laws that God gave the Israelites to govern the behavior of his people.

These prohibit certain acts that result from wrong thoughts: murder, adultery, theft and lying. God knows that rebellion begins in the minds of people, and that most of the time results in fatal consequences.

Like other codes of law of the ancient Middle East, the Ten Commandments not only condemn bad actions but also evil thoughts.

1 Kings 21:1-20. King Ahab and his wife Jezebel had broken the commandments of the Lord and lived in constant sin. Today's story tells about a tragic chain of events that began when King Ahab began to wish for the vineyard of a citizen named Naboth.

The vineyard of Naboth of Jezreel was next to the palace of King Ahab. The king wanted the property for himself and went to ask Naboth for it, offering Naboth another vineyard worth more money or whatever price the vineyard was worth. However, Naboth refused the proposal because the land was the inheritance he had received from his parents. He knew that if he sold it, he would be breaking the laws concerning inherited land.

The sad and angry king returned to his palace, lay down on his bed and would not eat any food. When his wife Jezebel heard why her husband was upset, she decided to plan the death of Naboth. She asked false witnesses to accuse Naboth of blasphemy and breaking the commandments of God.

The elders and rulers of the city, on the testimony of the two wicked men, found Naboth guilty and executed him according to the law: he was sentenced to death by stoning on the outskirts of the city.

Once King Ahab heard what had happened to Naboth, he went to take possession of the vineyard.

ADAPTATION

Television advertisements make every effort to convince us that we need everything that we see advertised and that we really want the new items that go on sale every season. Your students are easy targets for this kind of mental control.

Some people think that using certain products makes them more popular or more fun to be with. This can cause them to be frustrated when they do not possess everything they think they "need".

Students need to understand that evil actions usually start with wrong thoughts. Help them understand what it means to be greedy, and that they can fight bad thoughts and dishonest actions. Often, breaking one commandment means breaking others. It is a cycle in which there is no end. Help your students to be able to recognize when their thoughts can cause them problems.

LESSON DEVELOPMENT

Introduction

The Secret Sin

Lead a reflective discussion with your students and ask the following questions: "Do you think that you can break the law of God without performing an action? How do you think people do that?" (Allow time for them to respond.)

Guide the discussion to help your students understand that we do not necessarily have to do bad things, but sometimes bad actions come from bad thoughts. Sin begins in our minds.

Emphasize the idea that people generally think before they act, and God warns his children that bad thoughts can lead them to do bad things.

DEVELOPMENT OF THE BIBLE STORY

Write in big letters on the board or on a poster the word "greed". Ask your students if they know the meaning of this word and give them time to give their answers.

Tell them that greed is wanting something that belongs to someone else, and feeling angry or unhappy if they don't have it. Greed makes people feel jealous and angry.

The Bible story today is about greed. Tell them to pay close attention and look for the point in which greed enters into the heart of today's character.

Create a small skit based on today's story. Write a script for the four main characters: Ahab, Naboth, Jezebel and Elijah.

You will need four volunteers to help you by playing these characters, or if you have puppets available, use the puppets to tell the story to your students.

Give your volunteers the script that corresponds to their character ahead of time and ask them to study it during the week, so that on the day of class they are familiar with it and can concentrate on their voice tones to make the skit more interesting.

Create an environment that feels like you are in a theater. When the performance is finished, explain any questions your students may have and explain how it applies to our daily lives.

APPLICATION TO DAILY LIFE

Emphasize the idea that, like King Ahab, everyone feels greedy at times. But this is not pleasing to God, and he has given us a commandment that we must always obey.

Encourage your students to pray when they feel a thought of greed is entering their mind, and to trust that God will give them the strength to resist.

It is important to understand that their parents cannot give them everything they want, not because they do not love them but because they are not able to. They, as children of God, must learn to control their desires and be grateful for what they have.

ACTIVITIES

Naboth's Vineyard

Give your students the worksheet for this lesson, and let them number the pictures in the order that they took place in the Bible story.

Give a brief review of what they learned and go to the bottom of the worksheet.

Where Did It All Begin?

Ask your students, "When do you believe that greed entered the heart of King Ahab?" (Allow time for them to respond.) Refer to the footprints at the bottom of the worksheet. Point to the footprints in sequence and talk about the steps that Jezebel and her husband followed which lead them to invent the lies about Naboth that eventually killed him and allowed the King to steal Naboth's vineyard.

1. Seeing 2. Wanting 3. Coveting 4. Taking

Be A Superstar!

Help your students cut out the strip of stars from the CUTOUT Section of the activity books and provide them with glue.

Read the sentences on the worksheet out loud as students listen carefully, and have them glue a star in the white space next to each story that talks about a person who obeys the commandments of God.

MEMORIZATION

In a container place several pieces of paper containing the following instructions:

- ✘ Say the verse while jumping.
- ✘ Say the verse while crying.
- ✘ Say the verse while screaming.
- ✘ Say the verse while making a funny face.
- ✘ Say the verse while laughing.

Put the container in the middle of the room and have each of your students take a piece of paper. Have them take turns saying the verse while doing whatever their paper says.

Briefly review the unit that ends today, highlighting the truthfulness of God's commandments and the importance of following them.

CONCLUSION

End the class by reminding your students that we must respect the property of others and be grateful to God for the blessings He gives us. Pray for your students and invite them to come to the next class. If possible, give a short introduction to the next unit.

NOTES:

YEAR 1 UNIT III

THE STORY OF EASTER

Biblical Basis: John 12:12-19; 13:1-17; 19:17-42; Mark 14:32-42, 43-50; 15:1-20; Luke 24:1-12, 36-53.

Unit Theme Verse: *"But God demonstrates his own love for us in this: While we were still sinners, Christ died for us"* (Romans 5:8).

PURPOSE OF THIS UNIT

This unit will help your students:

- ✘ Know that God sent His Son Jesus to save the world.
- ✘ Learn the story of Easter.
- ✘ Celebrate that Jesus is Alive!
- ✘ Follow the example of Jesus by serving others.
- ✘ Communicate with God through prayer.
- ✘ Know that Jesus suffered by dying on the cross so that He could become our Savior.

UNIT LESSONS

Lesson 10: Jesus Came to Serve

Lesson 11: Jesus Prays in the Garden

Lesson 12: Jesus' Trial

Lesson 13: Jesus Died for Us

Lesson 14: Jesus is Alive!

WHY WE NEED TO TEACH THIS UNIT

Most of your students have heard stories about the meaning of Easter, the last supper, Jesus' prayer in the garden, the crucifixion and the empty tomb; but they need to understand the true meaning of what happened and why it is such a special time for Christians.

Through these lessons they will learn who Jesus is and the reason for his coming to this world. They will study the events in the life of Jesus, from his triumphal entry to the resurrection. They will know how the Son of God faced the crowds, the loneliness, the betrayal of friends, suffering and death. Through these lessons, they will have a broader and deeper understanding of the love of Jesus. They will learn about his dependence on prayer and his fervent desire to follow the will of God, his Father. This study will show them the reality of a living God who loves them and cares about them.

Your students will see the example of Jesus as he served, prayed and showed mercy; you will find opportunities to celebrate his resurrection and experience the forgiveness and mercy of God.

LESSON 10

JESUS CAME TO SERVE

GENERAL ASPECTS

Biblical Basis: John 12:12-19; 13:1-17

Memory Verse: *"But God demonstrates his own love for us in this: While we were still sinners, Christ died for us"* (Romans 5:8).

Lesson Objective: To help your students follow Jesus' example by serving the last supper to others.

TEACHER'S PREPARATION

The triumphal entry of Jesus into Jerusalem precedes the Last Supper. He entered the city on a donkey being welcomed by the crowd, who shouted, "Hosanna, Hosanna!! Blessed is he who comes in the name of the Lord!" and "Blessed is the King of Israel!"

When a king triumphantly entered a city mounted on a donkey it symbolized that they came in peace. Entering on a horse signified greatness and power. Jesus came riding on a donkey, a sign that he came in peace, even though the people wanted a military Messiah who would liberate them from Roman power.

People lost sight of the meaning of Jesus' peaceful entrance. And although he accepted the praises, the manner in which he entered denied his military ambitions.

The disciples had prepared the place for the Passover meal (John 13:1-17), and they arrived without washing their feet. It was customary for a servant to wash the feet of those who entered a house. This custom was necessary because, at that time, people walked barefoot or wore open sandals on dusty roads, so their feet were dirty and tired; after walking great distances, they would wash their feet to clean and refresh them.

When they arrived there was no servant to perform this task. It was impolite for people to wash their own feet, and the disciples did not want to or were unwilling to do that humiliating work; especially because they wanted to assume positions of power in the kingdom of God, which they believed Jesus was going to establish on earth.

Jesus knew about this conflict and, removing his cloak, he put a towel around his waist and washed the feet of each of his disciples. Peter was shocked, he could not believe that his Master was willing to wash his dirty feet, and he did not want Jesus to wash his feet. But Jesus insisted. When Jesus had finished this work, he asked them if they knew what he had done. With this act He gave them a lesson in service, not only because He washed their feet, but because of the attitude he had. He told them that if they served one another then they would be blessed.

ADAPTATION

At this age, it is common for students to think only about themselves. They find it hard to serve others. Through Jesus' model of serving others, students will see how the most important person, Jesus, became a servant to others. They need to understand that Jesus did this voluntarily. Help your students understand that they too can serve others.

LESSON DEVELOPMENT

Introduction

To illustrate this lesson you can bring photographs or magazine clippings of people who are helping others. Allow the students to describe the pictures and tell what they think about these people. Students have already formed a concept of who Jesus is; for them there is no doubt that he is the most important character in this story. You can expand this knowledge by telling them that he is the most important character in the history of mankind. In fact, years are counted before his birth and after his birth.

Added to that is the fact that He is the Son of God and that he is God made man (study more about the Trinity to explain this point.)

DEVELOPMENT OF THE BIBLE STORY

Using the introduction, say that Jesus is the most important man that has existed or will exist, and yet he gave us an example of service. Tell the story in an interesting way, highlighting the points that accentuate the purpose of the lesson. Sing songs with your students that have motions.

If you want and if it is possible, dramatize the foot-washing (for this you will need buckets of warm water and towels.) Narrate the story, and at the end ask your students to participate (those who want to.) Have them take their shoes off and then wash their feet in the water. After drying them with a towel, put their shoes back on them.

During this time, you can play appropriate background music; try to maintain an atmosphere of reverence and if you need to, ask for the help of some assistants. Give examples of people your students know who have the gift of service. This will help them better understand this act of humility. (They can be people of the church, in their school, community or country. Just make sure that the majority of the children know who you are talking about.)

Tell your students about a time when you helped other people and you were not ashamed to do so, but you did it out of an attitude of service. (You as a teacher are a role model for them, so your personal experience is very significant.)

APPLICATION TO DAILY LIFE

Throughout the lesson, the students must understand that no matter what position they believe they have in life (whether because of money, education, love in the family, etc.), none of them are more important than Jesus; he gave us this example and we must follow Him by serving others.

Ask your students, "How do you think you can help others?" (Some answers may be: Helping to clean the house, picking up the toys of others, sharing what I have, etc.)

Ask how many of them will take the challenge to be like Jesus Christ. Explain that we must follow his example of humility and service. Make it clear that we don't necessarily have to wash the feet of all the people we know, but we must be humble, and ready to help those in need.

ACTIVITIES

Jesus Gave Us an Example of Love and Service

You will need scissors, crayons, markers and an envelope for each child to store the pieces of the today's worksheet.

Tell students to color the worksheet and fill in the spaces of the verse with the correct letters. (Answer: example.) Ask, "What is happening in the picture?" (Allow time for your students to respond; expand on the information and take the opportunity to review the lesson.) Then, following the lines on the back of the worksheet, have them cut their worksheet into a puzzle. (Write their name on each piece, to prevent confusion with other students pieces.)

After they have cut the pieces out, ask them to mix their pieces up and then try to put their puzzle together again. After the activity, give each student an envelope so that they can take the pieces home. Encourage your students to share the puzzle with their family and friends and to tell today's Bible story to them.

MEMORIZATION

Cut out a large silhouette of a heart (it can be the size of a poster-board, preferably red.) Then write the verse on the heart; if it does not fit use both sides of the heart. Paste a picture of the crucifixion of Jesus on the heart.

Also prepare small hearts from the same material. Make one heart for each of your students and put their names on them. Tell them that when they can say the memory verse to you, you will place their heart on the board (or on a wall of the room); this will motivate them to learn the verse.

You can divide the class by gender and put up signs that say "boys" and "girls." As they learn the verse put their heart under the appropriate sign. Then give a prize to the group that learns the verse faster. Tell them that it is important to review the verse at home.

CONCLUSION

Help your students to gather everything that they should take home (worksheets, etc..) Thank everyone for attending today's class; share something from the next lesson that will make them want to come for the next class.

End the class as follows: form two circles (boys and girls) and assign a student in each circle to pray. At the end, you pray for everyone. Be sure to ask if they have prayer requests. Explain the importance of prayer and encourage them to pray every day.

NOTES:

LESSON 11

JESUS PRAYS IN THE GARDEN

GENERAL ASPECTS

Biblical Basis: Mark 14:32-42

Memory Verse: *"But God demonstrates his own love for us in this: While we were still sinners, Christ died for us"* (Romans 5:8).

Lesson Objective: To teach students the importance of prayer and that they can communicate with God through prayer.

TEACHER'S PREPARATION

The theologian Elwood Sanner gives us some interesting points of view about this passage. Jesus went to Gethsemane with his disciples, a garden that was on the Mount of Olives; a place Jesus often went to pray. Because it was nothing new, the disciples were not surprised that Jesus wanted to go there after the last supper. "Because the Lord kept vigil that night to bring them out of Egypt, on this night all the Israelites are to keep vigil to honor the Lord for the generations to come" (Exodus 12:42).

Knowing what was coming that night, Jesus felt the need to pray. He left eight of his disciples at the garden entrance and went with Peter, James and John on to Gethsemane; He wanted his friends close by while he prayed.

The impact of the cross began to preoccupy Jesus. Mark describes it with the strongest language possible: "My soul is overwhelmed with sorrow to the point of death," (Mark 14:34). The prayer of Jesus shows both his humanity and his love for God and his desire to do God's will. As a man, he wanted to escape the cross and the separation from the Father that this would bring; but as the Son of God, he must carry out God's plan.

The time for the sacrifice of Jesus was a few hours away; the horror and agony preoccupied him; he prayed an honest prayer for what he wanted: "Take this cup from me" (Mark 14:36). But he also prayed that the Father's will be done. The frustration and agony of Jesus was intensified when he found Peter, James and John sleeping. They were his closest friends on earth, and he asked them to pray and keep watch.

Again, he went away to pray and when he returned he found them asleep again.

ADAPTATION

Your students may not be accustomed to praying with much faith. It is very rare that they express their true and profound needs to God. There are two aspects that they can use in prayer: (1) To tell God what they want. (2) To accept the Lord's will for them. Perhaps they are only familiar with the former and not the latter.

It's good for them to begin to understand that prayer has the power to change us (character, attitudes). And through it, we can express to God our wants and needs. It's also important that they know that they can know what the Lord's will and direction for them is through prayer.

LESSON DEVELOPMENT

Introduction

It is likely that most students are not in the habit of praying except maybe at meal times and before going to sleep (and many not even at these times.) This lesson is very important to emphasize the importance of prayer in their lives.

Again, Jesus is an example to follow in this regard. Point out that during his life Jesus always depended on His Father and he was in constant communication with him. Ask, "How do you think that Jesus communicated with God? Did he do it by phone, by letter, or on the Internet?" (Let them answer.) "It was through prayer, which was vital during the most difficult moments of Jesus' life."

DEVELOPMENT OF THE BIBLE STORY

Be creative when you tell the story. Emphasize the pain and difficulty that Jesus faced in this situation. Ask your students what they do when they have pain or problems in their life (allow time for them to respond, most turn to their parents or friends.) Explain that Jesus went to God, His Father.

Emphasize the fact that Jesus was honest with God and did not hide his feelings. Encourage your students to do the same.

When we pray we should have confidence that God not only hears us but also understands us.

During the lesson you can include a short prayer. If you do, kneel down, put your hands together and pray there publicly (children learn more by example than by words.) At the end of the lesson have them pray in the same way. When you pray, use simple words that they understand.

APPLICATION TO DAILY LIFE

Having your students kneel in class and pray is a good start; however, you should encourage them to make this a habit, a way of life. Give your personal testimony about your personal prayer life (or you may invite the pastor or leader known in the local church, to explain how, where, when and for how long they pray.)

Explain to the students that prayer should be an important part of their lives and encourage them to put it into practice. Explain that you should start slowly, you do not have to pray one hour a day; they should begin with small goals that they can accomplish.

Take for example an athlete. Explain that today an athlete might run 42 kilometers, but they didn't get up one morning and say "From now on I'm going to run 42 Kilometers a day," and they began to run and they did it. No, on the contrary, they first decided that they wanted to run, and it is likely that the first day they only ran a short distance; but day after day they continued to run, adding a little more distance every day, improving every day to reach the goal they set.

Our prayer lives are like that athlete. We start with a short prayer, but as we continue to pray every day, our prayer time will get longer. Now is the time for your students to begin a life of prayer that will lead to great victories.

When Jesus prayed he didn't just tell God what he wanted. He also asked God to do in his life what God wanted to do. Tell the children that this is a good example of how to pray. They can honestly tell God how they feel and what they want. Prayer can help them accept the will of God, even when that is not what they want.

ACTIVITIES

The Prayer of Jesus

Hand out the worksheets for this lesson. You will also need markers or regular pencils, scissors, and glue or tape.

Read the prayer of Jesus that appears in the Bible story. Draw the children's attention to the statements on the worksheet. Read each of the statements out loud and together, as a class, decide whether it is correct or not.

If the statement is correct, have them circle it. Explain each of the statements to make sure the children understand them, especially the word "Abba". This expression is like saying "dad" or "daddy".

The Prayer Cube

Be sure to look over this activity before class in order to make it easier to help the students complete it.

Help your students follow the instructions and make the cube correctly. Explain the steps well as the wrong cut could spoil the end result (if you have assistants, have them make a cube and help the students with the process.)

When students have finished say, "This cube reminds us of some important things we need to remember when we pray to God."

Review each of the statements on the cube explaining in the best way possible so that each of the children understand them. Let them add comments as you discuss each of the statements; ask questions to find out whether or not they agree with what you say.

Do not forget to put each child's name on their cube to avoid confusion at the end of the class.

MEMORIZATION

If you used the system of the hearts for competition, begin by asking who learned the memory verse (probably none of them have learned it yet).

For this lesson, write the verse on the board and have the children repeat it; then erase some words and have the children say the verse including the words that were erased. Continue until you don't have any words remaining on the board. Finally ask who learned it and if they can say it, put their hearts in the assigned location.

CONCLUSION

Help your students to remember the things they should take home (worksheets, etc.). Thank each one for attending today's class; share something about the next lesson trying to get them excited so they don't want to miss.

Ask first a girl and then a boy to say a prayer of dismissal.

LESSON 12

JESUS' TRIAL

GENERAL ASPECTS

Biblical Basis: Mark 14:43-50; 15:1-20

Memory Verse: *"But God demonstrates his own love for us in this: While we were still sinners, Christ died for us"* (Romans 5:8).

Lesson Objective: To help students understand that Jesus suffered to become our Savior.

TEACHER'S PREPARATION

While Jesus woke his sleepy disciples in Gethsemane, the chief priests, teachers of the law, and the elders appeared with a large crowd. Judas had made arrangements with them to identify Jesus with a kiss, to let the authorities know they could arrest him.

One of the disciples, angry over the arrest of Jesus, drew his sword and cut off the ear of one of the servants of the high priest. The Gospel of John identifies this disciple as Peter and tells how Jesus miraculously healed this wounded man.

The painful prediction of the abandonment and desertion of his disciples came true. When they saw that Jesus did not resist the arrest and that no one from heaven came to his aid, they were frustrated. Was this the Messiah they were looking for? It was not a frustration of courage but of faith.

Early in the morning, the religious leaders brought Jesus before Pilate (Mark 15: 1-20). They had already judged him the night before, but because Israel was under Roman rule Pilate needed to pronounce the death sentence.

Pilate asked Jesus if he was the king of the Jews, to which he replied, "You have said so". Religious leaders continued to maintain their accusations against Jesus. Pilate asked him other questions, but Jesus was silent. And they made a disastrous mistake when they left the authority of the decision to the crowd. However, the final decision was Pilate's.

Pilate asked the crowd, "What do I do with this man they call 'the king of the Jews'?" The response from the crowd was not reliable, because the religious leaders had brought most of those who were present. The chief priests stirred up the crowd and asked Pilate to release Barabbas (a prisoner who had committed murder) in stead of Jesus.

For Jesus, the crowd shouted: "Crucify Him" Pilate lost control; He allowed Barabbas, a murderer, to be released; then ordered that Jesus be punished and be prepared for crucifixion.

The soldiers took Jesus into the palace mocked him, placed a purple robe on him and put a crown of thorns on his head. They started calling him "King of the Jews". Then they beat him and spat on him. Falling on their knees, they mocked him as if they were paying homage to him. Then they put his clothes back on and removed the purple robe. They had no idea how prophetic the mockery was for the character and mission of Jesus, because Jesus is King.

ADAPTATION

Students are still egocentric, so it is likely that they find it difficult to understand that a person is willing to suffer for them, as well as understand what their parents have been willing to suffer for their protection.

Hopefully, this lesson will help them understand why Jesus was willing to suffer for them long ago. They may see Jesus as a personal friend who cared so much for them that he was willing to suffer.

LESSON DEVELOPMENT

Introduction

Children are very sensitive to pain and suffering; use this to emphasize the pain and suffering that Jesus experienced during his trial. Not only was He sad because His disciples abandoned him, but also he suffered physical pain, his body went through the shock and pain of being beaten and he was ridicule. All because of his love for us.

Make your students aware that this was for each of them as well. Many do not feel guilty or included in this sacrifice, but this is your job, as the teacher, to help them experience and feel the pain of Christ's suffering.

DEVELOPMENT OF THE BIBLE STORY

For this lesson bring some pictures that show the passion of Christ. If your church has a television and

VCR or DVD, or laptop with DVD player available, project part of the movie "Jesus" (or another video that relates to this Bible passage) and show some scenes of Jesus' suffering.

If none of these are possible, then try to bring a whip to show your students what the soldiers used on Jesus. If you can't bring a whip, use photos to help your students understand the suffering that Jesus endured before he was put to death on the cross.

Be emotional when presenting this lesson; try to get your students to really understand the suffering and despair that Jesus felt.

Be sure to include songs or hymns like "On The Old Rugged Cross," or "At Calvary", etc.

Today's lesson is not a sad story from the point of view of the events that took place; but because of the abandonment of the disciples, the accusations, the trial, the hatred of the crowd (the same crowd that a week earlier welcomed him saying: "Hosanna! hosanna!" and spread their garments in its path) and the beatings it is very sad. But it is also a story of victory to see the triumph of love. Jesus did not opt for violence nor vengeance, his response was obedience and love for us.

APPLICATION TO DAILY LIFE

Students need to know that we are called to follow Jesus' example. In life, they will face situations where our first reaction will be to respond and defend ourselves, to attack or seek vengeance; It is likely that your students will face ridicule from their friends when they decide to do the right thing. Even in these situations, Jesus' example should serve to show us the right way to respond; be obedient and show love instead of hate.

ACTIVITIES

Why Did Jesus Suffer for Us?

Give each student the worksheet for this lesson, crayons, pencils, construction paper or cardboard, scissors, glue and transparent tape.

Allow time for students to describe what is happening in each of the pictures. (The first is Jesus' trial before Pilate, the second is when the soldiers beat him and the third is the crosses, representing Jesus being crucified and asking God's forgiveness for his enemies.) Each picture shows what Jesus suffered: he received unjust treatment and did not deserve what they did to him. However, he preferred to suffer so that we might have eternal life.

Ask your students how they think Jesus felt, and how they think they would feel if they received the treatment Jesus received and suffered the way he suffered.

Have the children draw a line to connect Jesus' response to the suffering of each drawing. Ask them to look up Luke 23:34 and read it together. Give them time to dialogue on this passage and express their feelings.

Memory Verse Poster

Be sure to do a sample of this worksheet before today's lesson; allow each student to take a large sheet of paper (12 x 8 cm) of their favorite color. Show them the example you've already made and tell them that this poster will help them to better understand Romans 5:8. Explain that there is no order to place the pictures in, but the words of the memory verse must be in the correct order.

Highlight the figure of Jesus on the donkey, Jesus washing the feet of his disciples, and Jesus on the cross. Explain that these are the ways in which God shows His love for us. Point out the figure of the empty tomb and tell them that this is the way God shows us his forgiveness.

Tell them that they should take the verse home with them and put their posters in their room, or somewhere in their house. This will help them to memorize the verse for this unit.

MEMORIZATION

If you are using the system of the hearts for competition, review with those that have already learned the verse. For this lesson, use the worksheet they did for review. Using your example, cover with a sheet of paper, portions of the verse, then ask your students to say the whole verse. Repeat by covering different portions of the verse.

Finally, ask who has the verse memorized and put their hearts into the assigned place to show that they've learned it.

CONCLUSION

Help the children to remember their things (worksheets, etc.). Don't forget to pray before leaving.

NOTES:

LESSON 13

JESUS DIED FOR US

GENERAL ASPECTS

Biblical Basis: John 19:17-42

Memory Verse: *"But God demonstrates his own love for us in this: While we were still sinners, Christ died for us"* (Romans 5:8).

Lesson Objective: To teach students that Jesus died on the cross in order that we might receive salvation.

TEACHER'S PREPARATION

Pilate ordered Jesus to be delivered to the execution squad, and carrying his cross, he left the palace and the city and traveled to a hill called Golgotha. Custom required that the condemned criminal carry his own cross. Jesus had already said: "Whoever does not carry their cross and follow me cannot be my disciple" (Luke 14:27).

And so they crucified him at Golgotha along with two criminals. Pilate had a sign placed on the cross proclaiming that Jesus was the "King of the Jews". This sign was written in the three main languages of the time, for everyone to read; Aramaic for local people, Latin for the officers and Greek for those of the Western Mediterranean world.

The inscription was used to identify the offense for which the victim had been sentenced. Proclaiming that Jesus was the King of the Jews had ironic implications; Not only was he the King of the Jews, he is the King of Kings.

When the soldiers crucified him, they took his clothes and divided them into four parts, one for each of them. The robe of Jesus was made of a special cloth and highly valued in those days. It was made with only one seam and it was one piece of cloth from top to bottom; so the soldiers decided not to split it and cast lots for it (John 19:24.) This happened so that the prophecy written in Psalm 22:18 be fulfilled, "They divided my garments among them and cast lots for my robe."

"Near the cross of Jesus stood his mother, his mother's sister, Mary the wife of Clopas, and Mary Magdalene" (John 19:25).From the cross, Jesus called his mother and John. In his agony, he showed compassion and affection for her.

ADAPTATION

It is difficult for your students to imagine death on a cross, much less understand. This lesson will create a bridge between the Old and New Testaments. Students will have new information about the sacrifice that Jesus made for humanity.

The expected response from students is to reflect on the bad things they know they have done. It's time for them to give thanks to God because of what Jesus did for them.

Some students maybe ready to accept Jesus Christ as their Savior, however, avoid pushing them. Let them respond in a deep and personal way to the news that Jesus suffered for them.

LESSON DEVELOPMENT

Introduction

Death is an aspect that children do not fully understand. Perhaps some of the class has experienced the death of a family member. For them, it is something undesirable and there is nothing positive about it. However, you must make them understand that Jesus' death was different, not only because it fulfilled the prophecies of the Old Testament but even more, because it had the character of sacrifice to pay for the sin of mankind.

DEVELOPMENT OF THE BIBLE STORY

For this lesson, bring photographs or pictures of graves in the cemetery and, of course, one of Jesus' tomb. Use this to highlight the contrast between the graves containing corpses and the empty tomb of Christ. Do not put much emphasis on the resurrection; this will be the theme of the next class; focus only on the fact of his death. Explain that this did not happen by accident or obligation, or because the Jews determined it. On the contrary, it was announced a long time ago.

Jesus knew what was going to happen. He agreed to be sacrificed for all of us; He did so knowingly and voluntarily. Finally, he died to make bridge between the Old and New Testaments, being the fulfillment of Scripture and prophecy.

APPLICATION TO DAILY LIFE

Your students need to know that the death of Jesus has implications for their lives. At this age, they have a poor concept of sin and spiritual responsibility. It is important that you as a teacher clarify that this sacrifice was also for them. They need to feel guilty about his death, but not in the sense of making them feel bad. This is important, because many believe they have nothing to do with the death of Jesus. They think it is for other people. Your students are at a difficult age, so it is important to face the reality of Jesus' death. This lesson will help you do that.

ACTIVITIES

The Ultimate Sacrifice

You need a worksheet for each student, crayons or markers, and scissors.

Ask, "What would have happened if the crowd had asked that Barabbas be sacrificed instead of Jesus?" Guide the discussion to the point of determining that Jesus would not have died. And although he did not deserve to die and Barabbas did not know of Jesus' great love, Jesus died in Barabbas' place.

Explain that God, from the beginning of the Old Testament, had warned mankind about the seriousness of sin and that the punishment for those that committed sin would be death, as God told Adam and Eve.

We know in the Old Testament and when Jesus was on earth, that people brought animals to the temple for the priest to sacrifice; this was how they showed God that they were sorry for having disobeyed him and that they did not want to die for it.

Although an angry mob killed Jesus, they could only do so because he allowed them to. And He not only took the place of Barabbas, but was also willing to be the ultimate sacrifice for the wickedness of mankind.

Let your students color and decorate the picture with the words, Jesus Forgives. Read Romans 5:8 and highlight the point that Jesus died for us, and that there is no need for sacrificing animals anymore because Jesus was the ultimate sacrifice.

The Cross of Christ

You need a worksheet for each student, scissors, and glue.

Be sure to make a sample at home before class starts today. Give each child a worksheet and allow them to make the cross by following the instructions. Use what you did to show how it should be done. Do not forget to have your students write their names on their work.

Use this activity to review last week's lesson, which has a direct connection to today's lesson. Tell your students when you see a cross remember that this is the symbol that for thousands of years has been used to identify Christians and that this symbolizes the sacrifice that Jesus made for us all. Make it clear that he did it because he love's us.

MEMORIZATION

If you used the system of hearts for competition, ask students who have already learned the verse to say it. For this lesson, use the large heart with the verse written on it. Sing a rhythm song that relates to the class. Ask your students to form a circle and walk around the classroom and when you say "stop!" have them all repeat the verse. Continue to do this several times. Finally, ask who has learned it and put their heart into the assigned place, to show that they have memorized the verse.

CONCLUSION

Help your students to remember everything that they should take home (worksheets, etc.). Thank everyone for attending today's class. Tell the something about the next lesson, so they won't want to miss class. Mention that next week will end this unit.

Encourage those who have not learned the verse to do so. Tell them that during the next class there will be an overview of the unit.

NOTES:

LESSON 14

JESUS IS ALIVE

GENERAL ASPECTS

Biblical Basis: Luke 24:1-12; 36-53

Memory Verse: *"But God demonstrates his own love for us in this: While we were still sinners, Christ died for us"* (Romans 5:8).

Lesson Objective: To help students celebrate that God raised Jesus from the dead and Jesus is alive.

TEACHER'S PREPARATION

The resurrection of Jesus and the coming of the Holy Spirit constitute the structure of the message of the entire New Testament, and the bases that enabled and strengthened the apostles to take the good news of the Gospel to everyone.

In almost all the situations where human beings came into face to face contact with celestial beings, one of the first reactions is fear. This happened to the women at the tomb. The angels asked them why they were looking for Jesus among the dead, and reminded them about the prophecies concerning his death and resurrection.

Even then, the women could not understand the wonder of it all. The apostles were somewhat confused with their reports; They had seen Jesus die a cruel death on that cross. But when the truth of the angels and the empty tomb penetrated their pain, they recalled the words of their Saviour; then they realized that the prophecies had been fulfilled.

All they had heard from their Master was fulfilled exactly. The misunderstanding and forgetfulness of the disciples contrasts to the memory of the Sanhedrin, who recalled that Jesus himself had said that he would rise on the third day, so they asked Pilate to place guards to guard the tomb.

Luke does not include all the details that are mentioned in the other Gospels; he makes a summary of the fact that the tomb was found empty and that the angels proclaimed the good news about the resurrection of Jesus. His aim was to proclaim the certainty of the resurrection.

Jesus is alive!

ADAPTATION

Your students have been hearing the events leading up to this lesson. Today they will learn that the love of God did not die with Jesus on the cross but rather extends to an empty tomb. That same love of the Lord still reaches us because Jesus lives today!

Kids like celebrations; they need to feel the same excitement you feel in telling this lesson. Make sure they understand that Easter is a celebration of God's love and it can be a very personal celebration for them.

In countries like the United States, it is celebrated with Easter bunnies, giving new clothes, looking for sweets, etc. This looks fun, but Easter is more, it is the celebration of God's love, the celebration of new life in Christ Jesus.

LESSON DEVELOPMENT

Introduction

If, in the last lesson you managed to create in the children a sense of personal value in relation to the death of Jesus, then now encourage them with the good news of his resurrection.

Make sure they understand the spiritual implications that this represents.

This is a lesson full of happiness and joy. Anticipate this by decorating your classroom. Make one or more large signs saying: "He Is Alive", "He Lives Today", "He Wants To Live In You" (trying to arouse interest in the children).

DEVELOPMENT OF THE BIBLE STORY

Start the introduction of the lesson in dialogue form, as if you are a reporter, talking as if the resurrection had happened today and the news is being transmitted (you can bring pictures of televisions, reporters, journalists, etc.).

Then have others act as journalists who will be narrating the news. To give it more impact, you can say, "News Flash! Jesus has risen! He fulfilled his promise of resurrection! He is not dead! The tomb is empty!" (Journalists can be several of the students, or invite young adults and teens from other classes.)

And in reality that's what happened. God gave a news flash to the disciples, it interrupted their normal life, and changed them forever.

After the dialogue, narrate the Bible story; do it in an entertaining and interesting manner. Be sure to include choruses with rhythm and movement, such as "God's Not Dead, He Is Alive," "Oh Happy Day" etc. or look for cheerful choruses. Remember that this is a lesson that transmits good news and joy.

Take advantage of the study of this lesson to ask your students if they want to accept Christ as their personal Saviour, and make this Easter the most special time of their lives.

APPLICATION TO DAILY LIFE

Today, God continues to give us this good news. And though it happened two thousand years ago, it still has the power to transform lives. And believe it or not, there are people who have never heard it, so it's a news flash for them; and if they hear it and understand it, it will change their lives forever.

If you have prepared questions, it's time to ask them. Bring candy or small gifts to motivate your students to respond correctly. Remember to ask simple questions with clear language.

ACTIVITIES

What Does Easter Mean?

You will need worksheets for each student, crayons, markers or colored pencils, and scissors.

In advance, make a sample of this activity so your students can see how it should look when it's done. Tell them to make two Easter cards, one for themselves and one to give to a friend or relative. (If you are making copies, be sure that you copy the front and back on the same sheet of paper or glue the two sheets together.)

These cards will help your students talk about the true message of Easter. Show them how the angel pops up after they have cut and folded the cards. Encourage them to color them and decorate their cards.

Use this activity to explain that the true meaning of Easter is the wonderful story of Jesus, his suffering, crucifixion and death. But above all, his resurrection. At this point, you can do a review of the entire unit.

MEMORIZATION

If you used the set of hearts for competition, start by giving an opportunity to the students that have not said their memory verse to say it for you. Allow your students to take home their hearts at the end of class, and help those who have struggled to say the verse.

Talk to the pastor of the church to see if your student can have the opportunity to share with the congregation what they have learned during the unit and their memory verse. They may also want to sing a song.

CONCLUSION

Help your students remember everything that they should take home (worksheets, etc.). Thank everyone for attending today's class; announces that the next class will begin a new unit.

If you want, let them take home some of the materials you used throughout the unit to have as souvenirs. Maybe for you they no longer have value; but for your students, they do.

Finish with prayer. Do not forget to ask if they have requests to include. If you want, have the children make a circle and ask for volunteers to pray. You should close in pray. In your prayer, thank God for sending His Son, Jesus Christ, who gave us an example of suffering, pain, service, and prayer. And most importantly, thank God for the resurrection of Christ, and the new life we can have in Christ.

NOTES:

YEAR 1 UNIT IV

TRUTH AND OBEDIENCE

Biblical Basis: Numbers 13:1-3, 17-33; 27:15-23; Joshua 3-4; 6:1-27; 1 Samuel 1:2, 21; 3:1-27; Nehemiah 1–4; 6 and 8; Ezra 7.

Unit Theme Verse: *"Trust in the Lord with all your heart and lean not on your own understanding; in all your ways submit to him, and he will make your paths straight"* (Proverbs 3:5-6).

PURPOSE OF THIS UNIT

This unit will help your students:

- ✘ Understand that God worked through men and women of the Old Testament that trusted him to fulfill his plans.
- ✘ Grow in the knowledge of God's greatness; and have confidence in the power he has to complete his plans.
- ✘ Be available to God and Trust in him and Obey him.
- ✘ Understand that trust and obedience are fundamental parts of our family, society, and spiritual relationships.
- ✘ Learn to trust that God can answer our prayers.

UNIT LESSONS

Lesson 15: Two Say "Yes" and Ten Say "No"
Lesson 16: A New Leader for God's People
Lesson 17: Joshua Trusts God
Lesson 18: When the Walls Fall Down
Lesson 19: Hannah Prays and Believes
Lesson 20: Samuel Obeys God
Lesson 21: New Walls for the City
Lesson 22: God's People Listen and Obey

WHY WE NEED TO TEACH THIS UNIT

Many of us have suffered bad experiences that have made us lose confidence in some people. Therefore, it is possible that we also have difficulty trusting in God. Teaching of this unit will help your students learn more about the power and grandeur of God; particularly his power to carry out his plans in this world.

The second emphasis of these lessons is that God doesn't usually work alone, he is looking for people to carry out his work, through actions of obedience from those who love and trust him. When we obey, our actions help fulfill His purposes.

When they hear the stories of Joshua, Hannah, Samuel, Nehemiah and Ezra students will discover more about the greatness and power of God. They will also see different ways in which the Lord works to fulfill his plan through people who trust and obey him.

Explain that the Bible does not tell about everything that happened with the people that are mentioned. Little is known of each of the situations they went through. However, the Bible characters had to trust in God every day, as we do today.

In this unit, your students will learn that God is always with us, helping us in many ways we do not even realize. When we trust in the Lord and do His will we are helping him do his work in this world. That is most important.

LESSON 15

TWO SAY "YES" AND TEN SAY "NO"

GENERAL ASPECTS

Biblical Basis: Numbers 13:1-3, 17-33; 14:1-35

Memory Verse: *"Trust in the Lord with all your heart and lean not on your own understanding; in all your ways submit to him, and he will make your paths straight"* (Proverbs 3:5-6).

Lesson Objective: To help students realize that when they trust in God and obey him, he gives them the courage to do the right thing.

TEACHER'S PREPARATION

God's plan was that the people of Israel would enjoy the Promised Land, a place where "milk and honey" flowed. He had done great miracles to bring them out of Egypt and to the borders of Canaan. But still the people lacked faith; They would not enter until they knew what the situation was there. The mission of the 12 men sent to spy out the land was not to see if they could conquer the land, because God had already told them that they would take it. Their mission was to collect information about it and its inhabitants, and set a route for the Israelites to follow when entering.

The report of the 10 men left no doubt that the land was good and it was worth going to possess. However, they worried that it seemed impossible to overcome the obstacles they would encountered to enter the land. But Caleb and Joshua had a totally different view. They too saw the walls and giants. However, they remembered that God had told them they would take the land. Their confidence in God was greater than their fear.

After the report of the 10, the people were full of fear, so much that they refused to enter Canaan. Their disobedience and lack of confidence angered God, who ordered that all men older than 20 years old would not enter the Promised Land, except Joshua and Caleb. The others would die while they were wandering in the desert for 40 years.

ADAPTATION

Friends have a great influence on children; and even when they know what is right, they often choose to do the incorrect thing just to be accepted by their friends. We need to help our students to know that they must do the right thing.

It is also important to learn to have more confidence in God; they know that only he gives them the strength to do the right thing. Joshua and Caleb decided to trust in God and obey him. That gave them courage. This is an example that we should follow.

LESSON DEVELOPMENT

Introduction

Getting to the Promised Land was what motivated the exodus of the people of Israel. Arriving at the Promised Land was the goal, the purpose of such a long and difficult journey. However, within walking distance of the Promised Land, they sent spies to explore it.

DEVELOPMENT OF THE BIBLE STORY

The report of the spies brought such despair to the people that they were seized by so much fear that they even wanted to return to the slavery from which they had been released. Emphasize how much effort it took for the Israelites to get there. You can include singing the song, "God Didn't Bring Us Here To Turn Back" (if you know it), or any other song that is appropriate. Keep in mind the purpose of the lesson as you tell the Bible story.

Use language that is clear and simple. Remember that most of your students don't know many Bible stories. It will be better if you use a version of the Bible in modern language to facilitate their understanding; if Biblical or religious terms are used, make sure that everyone understands their meaning.

If you can, bring a bunch of grapes, if not bring some grape juice (or some other fruit, honey, etc.). Use these to demonstrate how rich the Promised Land was.

APPLICATION TO DAILY LIFE

Use this lesson to help your students understand that many children their age do not like to do the right thing, on the contrary, most of them like to do what is wrong. But they have to make a personal decision, like Joshua and Caleb did, who choose to go against the majority in order to be obedient to God. Finally, highlight the fact that when we choose to obey God, he is grateful and will help us to obey him.

Encourage your students to follow the example of these two spies; encourage them to remember this story every time they are in situations where they have to make an important decision; especially when the choice is to obey and do the right then when their friends are challenging them to do something wrong.

ACTIVITIES

Who Saw What?

You will need your student worksheets, scissors, crayons, and an envelope for each child. Read the statements from the center of the worksheet; then discuss each picture with your class. Ask, "What do you see in these pictures?" (Lots of fruit, high walls, giants, flowing water) "Which pictures represent what the 10 spies saw and which represent what Joshua and Caleb saw?" Ask the questions on the worksheet and discuss the answers. Finally, ask, "What distinguished Joshua and Caleb from the other spies?" (They decided to trust in God. They wanted to obey his command to enter Canaan.)

Explain that to trust in God does not mean that Christians will never feel afraid; but rather than surrender to the fear they trust that God will help them. When we obey the Lord we are helping to carry out his plan. Let your students color the pictures and then have them cut out the cards and place their cards in an envelope with their name on it. Let your students take the cards home so they can tell the Bible story to their family.

Trust And Obey

You will need scissors, crayons or markers. Option: If you can, get clear plastic adhesive covers for light switches.

If you decide to have your students do this activity in class, follow the instructions on the worksheet; tell your students to color the light switch covers.

Read Numbers 14:9 (point to the upper left-hand side of the worksheet): "We have the help of our God. Do not be afraid!" Ask, Who said those words in the story today? (Caleb and Joshua.)They told the people to trust in God and he would give them the courage to do the right thing, even when everyone else had chosen to disobey the Lord.

If they don't do this activity in class, let them take it to make at home and bring it back finished to the next class.

Mention that these light switch covers can be put in any room of the house, so that they know that God is with them too. Remind them that when they trust in God, he is able to give them confidence so that they can do what God wants for them to do.

Tell them that in the next class you will ask them about difficult situations they have experienced during the week, which will help them to trust God more, because he gave them the courage to do so.

MEMORIZATION

Have all the children repeat the Bible verse together. Then divide them into 2 groups, boys and girls. Have each group repeat the verse. If you can, bring some visual aids to help them learn the text. (You could write it on a large piece of cardboard and paint it with several colors to make it more appealing. If you do not have the ability to make it, ask someone from your church to help.)

Ask the following questions about the lesson:

- ✘ How many spies were sent to explore Canaan? (12.)
- ✘ What was the report of the ten spies? (Good land, walled cities, giants, very dangerous, we cannot win.)
- ✘ What was different about the report of Caleb and Joshua from that of the other ten spies? (They said that God is with us, we can win, we will obey God.)
- ✘ After the Israelites heard the report of all of the spies, what did they do? (They cried all night, they wanted to return to Egypt, they refused to trust in God and they did not enter Canaan.)
- ✘ What happens when people decide to trust and obey in God? (They help in doing the will of God.)

Ask your students to come up with some ways that kids can show that they trust and obey God. (Accept any reasonable answer.)

CONCLUSION

Before the class ends, help the children to remember what to take home (worksheets, etc.). Thank everyone for coming and tell them something about the next lesson, trying to make get them excited about coming to the next class.

Finish with a prayer. If you want to, make two circles: one for boys and another for girls. Assign a leader for each circle to pray. Then you pray for everyone. Be sure to ask if they have any requests, and include them in your prayer.

LESSON 16

A NEW LEADER FOR GOD'S PEOPLE

GENERAL ASPECTS

Biblical Basis: Numbers 27:15-23; Deuteronomy 31:1-8; Joshua 1

Memory Verse: *"Trust in the Lord with all your heart and lean not on your own understanding; in all your ways submit to him, and he will make your paths straight."* (Proverbs 3:5-6)

Lesson Objective: To help students trust in God and obey Him, as they trust and obey the leaders that God has given them (parents, teachers, pastors, etc..)

TEACHER'S PREPARATION

After refusing to trust in God to possess the Promised Land, the Israelites began a pilgrimage of 40 years in the desert. During that time all men over the age of 20 died.

Throughout those years, Moses continued to lead the people of God. And when he was old, God told him it was time for the people of Israel to have a new leader. Maybe he was not surprised when the Lord chose Joshua as his successor.

From the time they left Egypt, Joshua had served Moses; he was also the commander in charge of the army of Israel. When others questioned the leadership of Moses, Joshua remained faithful. But more important than the position he had, it was that he was determined to obey God.

Joshua means "Jehovah saves." When this name is translated to the Greek, it becomes "Jesus," and there is an interesting parallel between this name and the name of the Son of God. Nothing bad is mentioned against Joshua; he was a person of good character and perseverance. He listened to the instructions from God and he complied with what was assigned to him. He wanted to know and do God's will. And when the Lord needed a new leader for his people, God chose him.

ADAPTATION

For various reasons, respect for leadership is unusual in many segments of society. Often, people see leaders as only seeking their own benefit and not the benefit of those following. This loss of trust is demonstrated often by criticism of leaders and their decisions.

Students have heard this kind of criticism, and learn these attitudes. Sometimes, they become disrespectful and lose trust in others. It is not good to tell our children that leaders are always right; however, we must help them understand that it is God who has given them the authority (Romans 13:1-7). For that reason, Christians are called to treat leaders with respect (Titus 3:1). The treatment of leaders in a disrespectful way is being disrespectful to God, since he has established authorities.

We respect the leaders of our church (1 Thessalonians 5:12-13). These people have special responsibilities to help build the kingdom of God. Respect and collaboration with the families of the church helps them to develop their work with greater efficiency.

LESSON DEVELOPMENT

Introduction

Moses' death was very sad for the people, but especially for Joshua, who was his servant for many years. However, God had a new leader for them. This lesson will help students understand that God changes leaders. That will help them understand that there may be changes in the church pastors or changes of teachers in Sunday school classes.

Emphasize that when a leader has to leave the church for whatever reason, God's work continues, it does not stop. The God who made Moses a leader is still alive, and is raising leaders today in the midst of his people, the church.

DEVELOPMENT OF THE BIBLE STORY

If you have access to the history of your local church, bring photos or information from some of the leaders who once were in the church (pastors, teachers, etc.) for this class. Tell students that to continue God's work on earth, the Lord needs leaders who are willing to obey and trust him.

Tell them that they are the future leaders of the church and society. Maybe God wants them to be future pastors and teachers, like you. You can include a personal testimony to enrich the lesson.

APPLICATION TO DAILY LIFE

This lesson is important, because not only must you teach students obedience and respect for leaders, but also make a double bridge between the leadership of past and current leadership, and at times, between the current leadership and future leadership. It is here where students are now.

It is good to ask what they aspire to be in the future. Make sure they understand that to become good leaders, they must first be good followers of God, as was Joshua.

ACTIVITIES

Respect the Leaders of God

You will need the worksheet and a soft ball. Ask the students: How did Moses, Joshua, and the people of Israel respect and obey their leaders? (Moses and Joshua obeyed the instructions God had given them. Joshua obeyed what Moses told him to do. The army was in agreement and listened to Joshua.)

Remind them of the promise that the army made to Joshua (Joshua 1:16-17). Ask, "Can you think of some reasons why the army would have difficulty trusting and obeying Joshua?" (He was a new leader. Moses was their leader for a long time and had also been a great leader. They did not know if Joshua would be a good leader.)

Say, "When the army decided to obey their leader Joshua, they obeyed and trusted that God had given them this new leader. How was their obedience to God's plans carried out?" (They served so that the people could enter Canaan, the land God had promised them.)

When we obey our leaders, we are obeying and trusting in God too. And so we are contributing so that the will of God may be done. Have the children turn the wheels they made on their activity worksheet. Say, Let's think about ways in which we can trust and obey God, and trust and obey our leaders.

Discuss the three figures that appear in the wheels using the following questions:

What is happening in this figure?

Are these children obeying their leader?

What makes you think they are not obeying?

(Answers. The children in figures one and two are being obedient. In figure three, you can give several answers as to whether the two children sitting together are obeying or not.)

Have them stand in a circle. Give one of them a ball and have them pass it between them. When you say "stop", they must do it. The child that has the ball must suggest a way in which they are able to show respect and obedience to our leaders. Repeat this activity several times. End the lesson by saying that God has given us our leaders, and therefore, we must respect and obey them, because by doing this we are also obeying and respecting God.

Before moving on to another section, review the lesson by asking the following questions:

- ✘ What promise did God make to Joshua when he chose him as the new leader of Israel? (That he would help him just as he had helped Moses.)
- ✘ What instructions did Joshua give to the soldiers? (That they should trust and obey the instructions from God.)
- ✘ What was the answer that the soldiers gave to Joshua? (We will obey you as we obeyed Moses.)

MEMORIZATION

Use the same text as last week. For this week, cut out the words of the text including the Bible reference. Repeat it several times; then ask for the collaboration of the children. Place all the words in a disorderly manner on a table; have everyone take a word. (If the group is small they will have to take two. If the group is large, you can do this in groups, so that everyone has the opportunity to participate.)

Then, ask them to stand and put the verse in order, allowing everyone to help verify the correct order. Once you have put it in order, repeat it again. To end, return the words to the table. (You can divide the group into boys and girls, and have a competition to see which group completes the text faster; if you decide to do this, cut out two sets of text.)

CONCLUSION

Conclude the class with prayer. Remember to thank God for the leaders you have had at the church, for those you have today, and of course, for the students who will be future leaders.

NOTES:

LESSON 17

JOSHUA TRUSTS GOD

GENERAL ASPECTS

Biblical Basis: Joshua 3-4

Memory Verse: *"Trust in the Lord with all your heart and lean not on your own understanding; in all your ways submit to him, and he will make your paths straight"* (Proverbs 3:5-6).

Lesson Objective: To help students trust in God and obey His Word, even if it is difficult for them.

TEACHER'S PREPARATION

They had already completed 40 years of walking in the desert when God brought the people back to Israel on the banks of the Jordan River. His plans for them were the same as before: enter the land of Canaan to possess it. That's what God promised Abraham hundreds of years before. Obeying His orders now would be as difficult as it was 40 years earlier; but perhaps even more because the Jordan River was more crowded.

Under the leadership of Moses, God revealed himself to the people through a cloud by day and a pillar of fire by night to guide them. Now the ark of the covenant was the visible sign of God's presence. The priests in charge of it carried it long distances in front of the people, and it symbolized the presence of God with them to guide them.

After reaching the bank of the Jordan and camping there, Joshua waited three days for God's instructions. Finally, he told the people to get ready, because the Lord had given them orders to follow; consecration prepared them for the wonderful power of God. This also showed their total dependence on Him. It also teaches us that only when we go to God and depend on Him can he do great things through us.

After the consecration, the people were ready to cross the Jordan. When the feet of the priests who carried the ark touched the water's edge, the river separated. The priests stood in the midst of this opening, and the people could cross over on dry ground. After all had crossed, Joshua appointed a representative from each tribe, and each one took a rock from the bottom of the river where the priests stood. They made an altar. This would serve as a sign to remind people of the power of God when they were obedient.

ADAPTATION

The Biblical story tells of the time when God used his power to help those who trusted in him and obeyed. Students need to know that almighty God, Creator of the universe, is interested in each of them. They should know that no matter the circumstance or situation where they are, they can to trust in God. This kind of trust is the foundation for obedience.

Obedience in practice helps us to strengthen our confidence. Thus, when we obey, we can see God working in our lives. Somehow the Lord allows us to help them complete their purposes on this earth.

Many students have not experienced demonstrations of the power of God. However, we can help them develop their confidence in Him by teaching the stories of God and His people, as the 12 stones reminded the people of the power of God (Joshua 4.)This teaches us and reminds us who and what God is.

LESSON DEVELOPMENT

Introduction

The miracle of crossing the Jordan River is the result of the commitment of the people to obey God through the leader that he had raised (Joshua). It was not the first time they had crossed water. With Moses, they had crossed the Red Sea. However, the people who were with Joshua were now a new generation; some were children; others were born after crossing the Red Sea, so this was just a story for them.

DEVELOPMENT OF THE BIBLE STORY

In developing this lesson, emphasize the fact that obedience made a miracle possible. Crossing the Jordan River in the conditions in which the people did was difficult, because it had overflowed. (It was the worst time of the year to try to cross the river.) This time, the people did not need to rush, and they were not pressured to cross like when they had crossed the Red Sea. When they had crossed the Red Sea, there was no other choice because Pharaoh was close behind them. However, the people obeyed Joshua and dared to trust in God.

Tell the story in creative ways. If you can, bring some elements of the lesson, such as water, sand, 12 stones. Emphasize the greatness of the miracle and the power that God has over nature. Finally, emphasize the gratitude of the people and the altar of 12 stones.

To begin, form a circle with the students and put 12 stones in the middle (if you can, make it like an altar). Then, ask what they think those stones represent. (Allow everyone to answer.)

Tell them that this lesson is about the 12 stones; ask them to sit down and start the lesson.

APPLICATION TO DAILY LIFE

Students should know that God is a God of miracles and that he still performs miracles today. But just like in the Old Testament, God still needs men and women, boys and girls who dare to believe in him. Let them see that they can be part of a miracle when they dare to believe in the Lord.

ACTIVITIES

Crossing the Jordan River

You will need the student worksheets, the correct page from the CUTOUT section, and scissors. Follow the instructions on the worksheet. Be sure that students understand the instructions. Have the materials ready beforehand, perforate the sections of the sheet where the illustration of the people crossing the river will be inserted. (It would be helpful if you use a knife to cut the slits before class time.) Ask, When did God stop the Jordan River? (When the priests touched the water with their feet.)

Read Joshua 3:15-16 and ask, What do you think would have happened if the priests had been afraid to trust and obey God's directions? (Maybe God would not have done the miracle, or God might have decided to wait longer to introduce his people to the promised land, like what had happened with Moses.) Why do you think that priests were willing to obey God's commands? (They had to trust in God, even when he asked them to do something dangerous and difficult.) What do you think people thought while crossing the river? (Accept responses.)

We Trust and Obey Today

Students sometimes face situations that are difficult for them. Think of some. Show children the figures on the worksheet. Let them see that at all times, even in special times, we must trust in God and obey him. Ask, Where or through whom can we find God's instructions for us? (In the Bible, a pastor, parents, a Christian teacher, friends and when God speaks directly to us.) Which of the pictures on your worksheet show times when we must trust and obey God? (The lower left and upper right pictures are routine actions.)

"Trust"

Have the children look at the back of their worksheets and begin a discussion by asking: "How can children show their trust and obedience to God in these situations?"

Possible answers: 1) Figure 1 - top left: By praying for someone who is sick. The Bible teaches us to pray for one another (James 5:14); but we must also follow the doctor's instructions. 2) Figure 2 - top right: By showing respect to those in authority (like teachers, parents, pastor, etc.), even though others do not want to obey; refuse to do evil even though others do bad things and ask you to participate.

3) Figure 3 - bottom left figure: You trust and obey God when you obey the instructions of your father to cross a street. In a violent neighborhood, you can trust that God will protect and guide you to make it all right.

4) Figure 4 - bottom right: By obeying the instructions of firefighters in case of a fire. We must trust in God even in difficult situations or whenever something bad happens to us.

MEMORIZATION

Cut out the silhouette of a big heart-preferably red. Inside it, write the memory verse. Also, write it in the area where the twelve stones are that you used for the class. Emphasize that by putting the Word of God in our hearts, we are reminding ourselves of God's power, just like the 12 stones by the Jordan River reminded the Israelites of God's power.

If you can and have time, prepare a small heart for each of the students. This will help them as they work on their memory verse at home. Ask them to draw an altar of 12 stones on the back of their hearts.

Please review the following questions:

- ✘ What promise did God make to the people the night before crossing the Jordan River into the Promised Land? (That he would do something amazing.)
- ✘ What instructions did Joshua give the people while they prepared to cross the Jordan River? (Look and follow the priests, keep away from the ark of the covenant.)
- ✘ What happened when the priests feet touched the Jordan River? (The river stopped flowing and the people could walk on dry land.)
- ✘ What did Joshua make with the 12 stones they brought from the middle of the river? (He built an altar.)
- ✘ Why did Joshua build an altar? (To remind the people and their future families of the miracle that God had done that day.)

CONCLUSION

Before finishing class, help students remember what to take home (worksheets, etc.). Thank them for coming and create anticipation for the next lesson, trying to make a connection and awakening interest for not missing.

Close with prayer. You can make a circle with the students and pray for them around the 12 stones. Do not forget to ask them to express their prayer requests and pray for them.

LESSON 18
WHEN THE WALLS FALL DOWN

GENERAL ASPECTS

Biblical Basis: Joshua 6:1-27

Memory Verse: *"Trust in the Lord with all your heart and lean not on your own understanding; in all your ways submit to him, and he will make your paths straight"* (Proverbs 3:5-6).

Lesson Objective: To help the students understand that they can trust in God's promises. That they learn to obey what God commands, even though this does not seem like a common thing to do.

TEACHER'S PREPARATION

When the 12 spies returned from Canaan, they all agreed that the cities were large, fortified, and walled. Joshua 6:1 says that the gates of Jericho were securely fastened. The inhabitants felt secure inside its walls; they did not know that this didn't constitute an impediment that could stop God's plan.

The instructions God gave Joshua to conquer Jericho surely sounded strange to the Israelite soldiers; however, they believed in the promise of God (v. 2) and were obedient: "I have given into thine hand Jericho." A convoy was formed: seven priests with trumpets of rams' horns, the ark of the covenant, Joshua and soldiers; all circled the city for six days. On the seventh day, they marched seven times and at the end, and at the sound of the trumpets, they all shouted. What a strange way to break down the walls of a city, don't you think?

However, the plan worked because Joshua and the people trusted in God and obeyed, although they did not understand the reason for the orders. God did what he had promised he would do.

ADAPTATION

Learning to trust in God has a direct connection with the act of learning to trust others. Adults sometimes ask students to do something they do not understand. When they ask why, we should help them understand what is the reason for the request; doing this will help them.

However, there are occasions when students should follow instructions given to them by those who are in authority over their lives, even if they don't understand the reasons. It is then where they should trust their parents or leaders, knowing that they know what is best.

When parents or leaders develop this kind of relationship of trust with students, this makes it easier to obey what they are asked to do, even if they do not understand everything.

When God asks us to do something, he doesn't always tell us why, and in these cases, it is more difficult to obey; however, we must always obey. Help the students understand that they can obey God without fear, confident that he knows what is best.

Today's lesson is a good example of this type of trust. The instructions God gave Joshua might seem even a bit ridiculous; However, his obedience and that of the people allowed God to fulfill his promises, and the walls of Jericho fell.

LESSON DEVELOPMENT

Introduction

The people of Israel had crossed the Jordan River and headed to take the first and most fortified city, Jericho. This was quite a fortress and its walls were famous for their imposing size. For this task, the people were not ready physically. Because of the time that they had been in the desert and the historical context, we can affirm that they didn't have much experience in military weapons and strategies. The only one who had actually been trained in this regard was Moses. He had grown up in Pharaoh's palace as a child and thus was educated at the military school of the Egyptians.

But Moses was not with them, and they had no weapons of war, since they had been limited to wandering in the desert. They had never established a place to develop an arsenal of war.

Emphasize how difficult this task was; how strange the instructions and how important it was to obey.

DEVELOPMENT OF THE BIBLE STORY

Prepare a dialogue to develop between two of your students or two volunteers. (It may be teenagers or young adults.) Prepare two outfits from Biblical times for use by the two characters (may be colored sheets or towels). The dialogue should be in writing. Do not forget to include the fact that the instructions were a bit strange to bring down such an imposing wall.

In this dialogue, one of the soldiers must be incredulous and the other should give confidence; one should emphasize how difficult the task, the other on what God has provided and that we can trust him even if his instructions do not seem so logical.

Make sure that the dialogue is neither long nor short. Make it suitable to be part of the lesson, and allow the volunteers or invited guests to develop it. At the end, tell the Bible story; emphasizing the purpose of the lesson. Repeat the words that emphasize the teaching goal, such as trust, faith, obedience. If you can, write them in large letters and stick them on the board or on the nearest wall.

During class, carefully observe the children and see the expressions on their faces. This will give you an idea of how they are responding to your words. Emphasize that we all have walls in our lives which seem impossible to break down, but if we learn to trust and obey God, those walls will fall like those of Jericho. (Mention walls as enemies, pride, problems family, etc.)

Finish the lesson by asking the following review questions:

- ✘ What is the name of the first city that God told the Israelites to take? (Jericho)
- ✘ What did God tell Joshua and the people they should do for six days? (March around Jericho once a day, without saying anything.)
- ✘ What did the priests do when the people finished the seventh lap on the seventh day? (They blew their trumpets.)
- ✘ What did the people do when he heard the trumpets? (They shouted.)
- ✘ What happened to the walls of Jericho when the people shouted? (They fell.)
- ✘ What would have happened if Joshua and the people of Israel had not obeyed God? (The walls of Jericho would not have fallen.)
- ✘ Finish with this prayer: The story of Joshua and the wall of Jericho teaches us that we must obey God's commands, even if we don't fully understand his reasons.

Conclude by repeating the objective of the lesson. Remember in each class to include songs with movements. They can sing the chorus: "The Israelites circle seven times around Jericho," or some other similar chorus. As they sing, have them circle seven times around the classroom.

In daily life, it is the same. There are orders and rules, that even though we do not realize, they are there and we must obey. For example, although it is not written on each street, we know that there are standards for vehicles and for pedestrians. If we walk in the middle of the street, we could have problems and even be killed.

Students must recognize that we live in a world full of orders and rules to be obeyed, which they consciously or unconsciously have been obeying since birth. In each household, you eat at a certain time. We cannot come and demand to eat when that time has passed. Emphasize this in order for students to understand that obedience is part of life. Let them give some examples in this regard.

APPLICATION TO DAILY LIFE

This lesson should help students recognize that obedience is essential in life, not only within the church and in our relationship with God, but also in life in general. At home, we must obey the orders and rules of our home. The same at school: we must obey orders and rules. Therefore, we cannot ignore or disobey them, because if we do, we will have consequences to pay.

ACTIVITIES

Mystery Puzzle: Trust - Obedience

You will need scissors. (Optional: crayons or markers, cardboard and glue.) Help the children cut out the puzzle and find the message from their worksheet. Whoever wants to can color their puzzle. To make it stronger, paste the worksheet on cardboard before cutting it out; this will make the pieces thicker and stronger.

MEMORIZATION

Write the memory verse on the board and repeat it three times. Erase some interspersed words; repeat the verse two more times. Then, erase other words and repeat it two more times. Now, write it all again and erase different words and do it again. Continue this process until you no longer have any words on the board.

Just for fun, have your students march seven times around the classroom, repeating the verse as they march. Then have them sit down in order as they finish the last lap to simulate the fall of the wall.

CONCLUSION

Thank each of the children for attending class. Create anticipation for the next lesson, try to make a connection and awaken interest for not missing. Close with prayer.

Do not forget to ask for prayer requests and include them.

LESSON 19

HANNAH PRAYS AND BELIEVES

GENERAL ASPECTS

Biblical Basis: 1 Samuel 1:1-2, 21

Memory Verse: *"Trust in the Lord with all your heart and lean not on your own understanding; in all your ways submit to him, and he will make your paths straight"* (Proverbs 3:5-6).

Lesson Objective: That students will learn to trust that God can answer prayers in the best way possible.

TEACHER'S PREPARATION

Hannah was the wife of Elkanah, but not the only one. As in other cases in the Bible, marriages of this type caused problems. Elkanah's other wife was called Peninnah. She had children, but not Hannah, which was frowned upon in that society. However, this did not affect the love Elkanah had for Hannah. Even though she had no children, he preferred her to Peninnah. At that time, to have a son was to honor her husband. And for Hannah, the inability to give Elkanah a child caused her great pain.

When they made their annual trip to Shiloh to worship, Hannah asked the Lord fervently to give her a son. To show the Lord that her request was not a selfish thing, she offered to dedicate him to his service.

When God answered her prayer and gave her a son, Hannah remembered her promise. When Samuel was ready, Ana brought him to Shiloh and presented the boy to the priest, Eli, to serve the Lord in the tabernacle.

Hannah's prayer of thanks is located in Chapter 2 of 1 Samuel and is known as the "Magnificat" of the Old Testament. Her overflow of praise to God is very similar to the prayer of Mary in Luke 1. God was pleased with Hannah and honored her with three more sons and two daughters.

Hannah did not forget her child while the child grew up under the supervision of Eli. Each year, she made a new robe for her son and she brought it when the family went to Shiloh to worship God.

ADAPTATION

Many students, perhaps the majority, still pray focused on themselves; maybe some have progressed to the point of saying, "God is great, God is good." In most prayers, they thank the Lord for what he has given, or answers to their requests. That does not mean they are not praying; however, they can learn to pray a more significant prayer if an adult teaches them.

Help your students understand that God can speak freely on any matter. This includes thanks for what you have, making personal requests, and anything else.

Students need help to understand that when they pray, they must ask God to do His will; in this way they will accept the Lord's answers to their prayers. This is not an easy lesson to learn, even for adults.

LESSON DEVELOPMENT

Introduction

Ask students what they know about prayer. (Let them respond.) Invite one or more volunteers to come to your class and share with the class about an experience when God has answered their prayer(s). Say, "We can pray to God anytime and talk about any subject." Then ask, "When do you pray?" (Before eating, at church, before bed, etc.)

When we pray, we must believe some principles about God. Make three statements and ask the children to raise their hands if they agree with each.

1. We believe that God hears us when we pray.
2. We believe that God can answer our prayers.
3. We believe that God wants the best for us.

Say, "In the Bible story today we will learn more about prayer. After the lesson I will ask you some questions about these three statements."

DEVELOPMENT OF THE BIBLE STORY

In advance, find a plastic baby or doll. Get different colored clothes to dress it. Emphasize the fact that Hannah prayed and believed in God. To tell the story, bring to class this doll, in order to emphasize the fact of leaving Samuel at the temple at a very young age. If you have several types of clothes, show that Hannah visited her son each year and brought him a different robe.

In developing the class, take into account the amount of time that students can pay attention. Tell the story in a pleasant and interesting way. If you see that they do not pay attention, do not rush to finish the lesson, better use a song with movement and then continue.

Remember that the success of the class depends on your preparation.

Finish the lesson by asking simple questions such as:

- ✘ Why was Hannah sad? (Because she had no children.)
- ✘ What did Hannah do when she and her husband Elkanah went to Shiloh to worship God? (She prayed and asked God for a son.)
- ✘ What promise did Hannah give God if he gave her a son? (That she would give her son to serve in the house of God forever.)
- ✘ What did Eli the priest say to Ana when he heard her request? (Go in peace, and may God hear your prayer.)
- ✘ How did God answer Hannah's prayer? (He gave her a son, Samuel.)
- ✘ True or False: Hannah kept her promise and gave Samuel to serve God forever. (True.)
- ✘ What can we say to God when we pray? (Anything that is important to us.)
- ✘ What are the three ways in which God can answer our prayers? (Yes, no, wait.)

APPLICATION TO DAILY LIFE

This lesson is good because it highlights the power of prayer. Briefly, explain to students that prayer is talking to God, it is not repeating meaningless words without feeling.

Emphasize that when we pray, we have the confidence that God hears us and is able to answer our prayer; but will respond in the best way for us. Belief is the key point. Students are at a critical stage of life in relation to belief. They are leaving the stage of childhood where they believe everything (belief in Santa Claus, Superman, Spider-Man, etc.). At this stage of life, they realize that many things they took for granted as a child are now questionable and some of them have proven to be lies. This brings a chain reaction that leads them to an attitude of total distrust. This, of course, includes the spiritual realm. Some of them are beginning to question the existence and power of God.

It is vital that you pray for your students and ask God to give you wisdom to address these issues. You as a teacher play a critical role in the spiritual life of students.

ACTIVITIES

Yes, No, Wait

You will need the worksheet, crayons and markers.

Ask, What does Psalm 4:3 say God will do when we pray to him? (Hear us.) Does this mean that God will always do what we ask? (Let students respond.) Explain that God always hears and answers our prayers; he answers giving us what is best for us. Sometimes he says "yes"; other times he answers us with a "wait"; and other times "no".

We can talk to God about anything. We need to trust that he will answer our prayers according to His will and what it means for us. No matter his answer, we should always praise him for having listened. God loves us and wants to hear.

Focus the attention of students in the final part of the worksheet, on the traffic lights. Explain that after reading every situation, they must decide the color of the light that best suits the situation. The color red is to say "no," yellow is to say "wait" and green for saying "yes." Suggest the answers without being rigid. Some students may have different answers. Let them explain why they think so, and correct them when necessary without offending or upsetting the student.

Shhhh, I'm Praying

You need the top part of the two worksheets, scissors and glue. (Optional: clear contact paper and crayons.)

Have the children cut out the two upper parts of the worksheets (door hangers). Allow them to decorate them. Then, you can cover it with clear contact paper to have greater protection.

Tell them that this is to hang on the door of their room to let others know that they are praying. When they stop praying, turn it over so you see the phrase "God Listens To My Prayers."

Psalms 4:3

You need the worksheet and pencils.

Let your students put the correct words in the crossword puzzle. Then have them write the correct words on the blank lines to complete the verse.

MEMORIZATION

You can use any of the methods mentioned in previous lessons, or find a creative new way to teach the memory verse.

Help them to remember everything they need to take home (worksheets, etc.). Thank everyone for attending class and make some kind of connection to the next lesson.

CONCLUSION

Close with prayer. Have three or four volunteers pray for something or someone else. End this time thanking God for hearing our prayers and answering with what is best for us.

LESSON 20

SAMUEL OBEYS GOD

GENERAL ASPECTS

Biblical Basis: 1 Samuel 3:1-27; 7:3-17; 8:21; 9:16-17

Memory Verse: *"Trust in the Lord with all your heart and lean not on your own understanding; in all your ways submit to him, and he will make your paths straight"* (Proverbs 3:5-6).

Lesson Objective: To help students understand that God speaks to those who hear his voice and obey.

TEACHER'S PREPARATION

Samuel is someone who we can call a "miracle baby," because he was a response to the prayer of his mother. While still a child, his family took him to Shiloh so that he could stay to live with Eli, the priest. This was to fulfill the promise that his mother had made to God that when the child was born, she would dedicate him completely to his service.

When Samuel grew up, he learned to help Eli in several components of the Tabernacle. It was there that he received his education. His sensitivity to listen and obey the voice of God began when he was just a young man. He heard the Lord's voice calling him to give him a message to Eli. And even when the message was judgment, Samuel told all that God asked him to tell; he did not remain silent.

Samuel lived in a time of transition in the history of Israel. The era of the judges was reaching its end, and the time of kings was about to begin. Because of his faithfulness to hear the voice of God, the people trusted that Samuel could be relied on for guidance. When God chose a leader, Samuel received his instructions to give to the people.

ADAPTATION

Students are old enough to take responsibility. They want to be "big" and "independent"; what they do not understand is the more independent they will be, the more responsibility they will have.

Samuel heard the voice of God when he was a child, and did what he asked him to do. That sensitivity at such a young age to hear the voice of God established the parameters for life.

Listening often requires effort and concentration. Students easily forget what their parents or other elders tell them. The same applies to parents. Sometimes, they also forget what their children told them.

It is not easy to develop listening skills. Help students realize that they may more easily develop some skills because they are young. They are ready to hear the voice of God. No need to wait to be adults for that.

Highlight the fact that God speaks in different ways to let people know what is his will. Emphasize that he is always with them and helps them do the right thing.

LESSON DEVELOPMENT

Introduction

From the time he was very little, Samuel learned to listen to the voice of God. This is a very important detail for students, as they often think they are too young to be involved in the things of the Lord. Emphasize that Samuel grew up in the temple, and that is an example that they can follow. Age is no barrier to have a personal relationship with God and to hear his voice.

DEVELOPMENT OF THE BIBLE STORY

For this lesson, you can bring a blanket or a small cushion to dramatize when Samuel was sleeping and heard the voice of God. Ask a volunteer to lie down and pretend to be asleep. Then call him by name, saying that today's lesson is about someone who was sleeping and heard a voice.

Emphasize obedience, because the message that Samuel received was not an easy message to deliver because he liked and respected the priest, Eli. However, he obeyed and delivered the message as it was and as God asked him to do it. Make the connection to last week's lesson reminding your students that Samuel is the son of Hannah.

Highlight the fact that God speaks to us in many ways. Talk about some of these ways with the class, so they know how and where to listen for the Lord's voice.

APPLICATION TO DAILY LIFE

Sometimes, to say or do the will of God is not easy, especially when it involves our own family or leaders.

Yet, we are called to say and do the right thing, and God can use us in that. Samuel's case is an example. Eli was almost like a father to him, and he could only see his family once a year. To comply with the message that God gave him was not easy.

Sometimes students see their parents or leaders do wrong things, creating in them a conflict to confront them or not in some situations. Guide them in the sense that they can speak frankly when they think something is wrong, but they should never disrespect anyone. When Samuel spoke with Eli, he did it with respect and love. This must be the right attitude in circumstances such as these.

If you feel this application will bring more problems than solutions, then guide the attention of the class to the fact of the different ways in which God speaks. Pray that the Lord will guide you in this regard.

ACTIVITIES

Trust in God to Do it Right

You will need your student worksheets, pencils or pens. Allow the children to use the code on the worksheet to finish the Bible verse. When they have completed the verse, repeat it together. Option: Choose a volunteer to tell you what a letter should be. Allow all the children to participate. Ask them to look at the completed verse; say "This is a prayer to God." Ask, "To whom is the writer speaking?" (To God) "What is the writer asking?" (To teach and to guide them.)

How Does God Speak?

You will need: scissors, glue or tape, drawing paper, crayons or markers.

Make an example of this activity so your students can see how it should look. Teach it to the students and tell them, "Let's talk about some ways that God communicates with us today." Have the children take the worksheet and discuss what is happening in the different pictures; let them tell how God could speak to us in each of the examples. Discuss each picture or situation as much as you feel your students need.

The situations depicted in the pictures for discussion are:

- Music/Singing.
- The Bible.
- Christian Books.
- Preaching.
- Teacher in Sunday School.
- Prayer.

Ask, How does God speak to people? (Through a hymn or through reading His Word. The music serves to praise him. The Bible teaches us the right way to live. Prayer helps us to know what God wants us to do. Sunday school teachers and pastors can have lessons or messages that people need to hear to encourage them to change their life.)

Talk about Samuel and his response to God. He said: "Speak Lord, your servant is listening" (1 Samuel 3:9). Say, "We have studied the different ways in which God can speak to us. When he speaks we must listen." Give each student a worksheet and have them cut along the solid black lines and fold on the dotted lines. This will form a window. Then glue a blank piece of paper to the back of the worksheet, so it shows through the opening. (Note: Do not glue the area of the window, as this should be free to open.) Then, have your students draw a picture showing how God can speak to them. Now when they open the window, they will be reminded of how God speaks to us. Finally, encourage your students to listen and obey the voice of God.

MEMORIZATION

Write on different cards the words of the memory verse. Before students arrive to class, hide them (you can tape them under chairs, on the back of the door, etc.). When it's time to say the verse, tell your students that Samuel thought it was Eli who first spoke to him. It was later that he could tell it was the voice of God. Somehow God's voice was hidden the first time. Tell them the memory verse is hidden in the classroom, and the task is to find the words and put them in order. Once they have found all of the cards, have them put them in order, and repeat the verse several times.

CONCLUSION

As in previous classes, help students not to forget anything that they must take home (worksheets, etc.), and thank everyone for attending today's class. Create anticipation for something from the next lesson, trying to make a connection and awakening interest for not missing.

Conclude with a prayer; thank God for the way he communicates with us and pray for students to have that kind of experience. Do not forget to ask if they have prayer requests and include them in your prayer.

LESSON 21
NEW WALLS FOR THE CITY
GENERAL ASPECTS

Biblical Basis: Nehemiah 1–4, 6

Memory Verse: *"Trust in the Lord with all your heart and lean not on your own understanding; in all your ways submit to him, and he will make your paths straight"* (Proverbs 3:5-6).

Lesson Objective: To help students learn to trust in God. He always provides what we need to accomplish His will.

TEACHER'S PREPARATION

The time between the Biblical story of Samuel, Ezra and Nehemiah is longer than the period of time between Joshua and Samuel, that is about 400 years. While Samuel, Ezra, and Nehemiah were another 600 years. Ezra and Nehemiah are located within the "classical" period of the prophets. Israel had made progress in some areas and had receded in others. Throughout Biblical history, there is a relationship between obedience and trust in God. He always wants the best for his people, and that they trust and be obedient to His Word.

ADAPTATION

Students like to be part of what is happening around them. Their enthusiasm is often greater than their abilities. With the help of someone, they can do a lot for the service of God. You should teach them that the Lord's power will always be available, and they do not depend only on their own strength.

Explain to them that, although we know what God wants us to do, that does not mean that it will be easy to do. We need to trust that he will help us to fulfill his purpose.

Nehemiah discovered that this was true. Although he was sure he was doing the will of God, he faced opposition. However, he trusted in God and he finished the work entrusted to him.

LESSON DEVELOPMENT

Introduction

In Biblical times, the city walls signified security. They served not only as decoration but were a necessity. Hence, the urgency to rebuild. Tell students that God provided what was necessary to do the work. If you can, take some building materials to class (hammer, bricks, etc.). Use this as supporting material for the lessons.

DEVELOPMENT OF THE BIBLE STORY

Although Daniel 9:2 says that the desolation of Jerusalem would last seventy years, it took many years to rebuild. Jerusalem had remained in ruins since the Babylonians had taken the city. The desolation lasted for seventy years, as God had told Daniel. However, the city was still in ruins 60 or 70 years after the desolation; only the poor had remained in the country; the others had been taken captive to Babylon.

Later, the Persians defeated the Babylonians, and the leaders of the Israelites were taken to Persia. Some of the exiled Israelites returned to Jerusalem, but they weren't able to reconstruct the walls of the city.

Nehemiah heard that Jerusalem was still in ruins (chapters 1-4, 6) and determined that he should do something about it. He prayed to God about this and when the opportunity arose, he spoke to the king.

God prepared Nehemiah for this mission, allowing him to have an important position as a cupbearer to the king (serve him wine in his glass). This place was more than a mere servant, also he was a counselor. One of the requirements for access to that post was that the person was always cheerful before the king.

The king saw the sadness of Nehemiah and asked for an explanation. He told the king about the destruction of Jerusalem and asked if he could travel to Judah to supervise the work of rebuilding the walls. The king not only authorized him to go, but also gave him letters of protection for travel and supplies.

When Nehemiah arrived in Jerusalem, he found that the situation was worse than imagined. People were discouraged and believed that there was no use in rebuilding the walls. Nehemiah encouraged the people and organized them to work in teams. Each family was assigned to work on a section of the wall near where they lived. All the people were involved and motivated to work.

They heard rumors that there would be an attack on the city. Nehemiah divided the group into workers and guards. The guards watched with sword in their hands; workers worked with the sword at their side. And so they continued the task.

With the Lord's help, they rebuilt the wall in 52 days. Israel completed the task in such a short time that even their enemies knew God had been with them helping them.

APPLICATION TO DAILY LIFE

Your students need to know that there are walls that need to be rebuilt in their lives. These can be in the family or some spiritual or emotional area. Assure them that if they trust God and obey Him, He will provide what they need to rebuild those walls in their life.

ACTIVITIES

Nehemiah Rebuilds the Walls

You will need the worksheet, two sheets from the CUTOUT section of stones, and glue.

Allow students to cut out the stones from the two CUTOUT pages. Help them find the correct statement that corresponds to each statement from the worksheet. Then, allow them to glue the stones onto the worksheet. (The answers are: 1) Servant of the king. 2) The walls of Jerusalem were destroyed. 3) let him go and build new walls. 4) the enemies tried to stop him. 5) the people worked together.

After the children have completed their work, ask these questions:

1. In this story, what do you think God's plan was? (That his people would have the protection and security of the walls.)
2. What did Nehemiah want do to fulfill God's plan? (Work with the people and rebuild the walls.)
3. Why were Nehemiah and the people able to rebuild the walls so fast? (Because they trusted God, they worked together and God helped them.)
4. What would have happened if they had not wanted to work together? (The walls would not have been rebuilt and they would not have done the will of God.)
5. In your own words, tell the class what God teaches us in this lesson. (We should work together and God helps us when we trust and obey.)

I Can Help Do the Work of God

You will need cut-outs of the church from the CUTOUT section, scissors, glue, pencils or pens.

Have the children cut out the pieces of the church, from the same sheet that they cut stones for the work of the walls. Then glue them in the appropriate places.

Say, "Nehemiah asked God to help him rebuild the walls, and he did what the Lord asked him to do. We can also help God to do his will. Let's talk about some activities that we can perform. Let's start with the roof of the church. What does this part say?" Let children respond. "Yes. Worship. How does worshiping God help the church fulfill His will?" (Worship honors God and our love becomes stronger for him. It reminds us to trust and obey the Lord to do His will.)

Continue in this manner until you reach the center of the church. When finished ask, "Can you think of any other way we can do the will of God?" (List the suggestions of the children on the blackboard. Possible answers: Pray, give, send cards to those who missed Sunday School, visiting the sick, helping the elderly, singing in the choir, helping at the church, invite a friend to class, etc.) After making the list, ask the children to choose two of the options and to write them in the bushes that appear on each side of the church.

You Decide

Direct the attention of the children to the picture that is on the right side of the church that they just finished. Highlight the fact that Nehemiah did the will of God even though some people tried to stop him. Sometimes people try to stop us and we do not do the will of God. Read the dialogue between the children and discuss the questions. (Answers: 1. No, it is not bad to play ball, but it is wrong to break a promise to be able to play. 2. It may be hard for the child to stop playing, especially if they love to play and do not really enjoy helping with the garden. 3. Remember that God will help you when you're determined to obey. Remember the story of Nehemiah and the wall.)

MEMORIZATION

You can use any of the methods mentioned in the previous lessons or find a creative way to teach the memory verse.

Help students to remember the things they need to take home (worksheets, etc.). Thank them for attending class; create anticipation for the next lesson, trying to make a connection so they won't miss the next class.

CONCLUSION

Before leaving, ask students to stand in a circle. Ask for a volunteer to do the closing prayer.

LESSON 22

GOD'S PEOPLE LISTEN AND OBEY

GENERAL ASPECTS

Biblical Basis: Ezra 7; Nehemiah 8

Memory Verse: *"Trust in the Lord with all your heart and lean not on your own understanding; in all your ways submit to him, and he will make your paths straight"* (Proverbs 3:5-6).

Lesson Objective: To help students understand that Jesus suffered to become our Saviour.

TEACHER'S PREPARATION

In the Hebrew Bible, the books of Ezra and Nehemiah were one, which was called the "Book of Ezra." In our Bible, this book contains distinctive narratives: (1) From Chapter 1 to 6, the return of some Israelites to Jerusalem under the leadership of Zerubbabel and the rebuilding of the temple. (2) From Chapter 7 to 10, the second return under the leadership of Ezra with great help from Nehemiah, who arrived later. In between events there is a silent period of 60 years.

Ezra was a scribe and priest who lived in Persia. King Artaxerxes greatly rewarded him. (He is very likely to have given him a high position in his court.) One day he asked the king to permit him to go to Jerusalem on a mission of teaching, and he not only gave permission but let all Israelites in his kingdom, including priests and Levites who wanted to go join him (Ezra 7:13). In addition, he gave authority from him and his court to act as a messenger and inquire about Judea and Jerusalem (Ezra 7:14).

Fifteen hundred men took advantage of this opportunity in the second return. With their families and servants, the number reached about five thousand people. To reach Jerusalem, the exiles had to walk 1,500 km. The trip took them four months.

Even in exile, Ezra was a serious student of God's law. He believed that the people should hear it. Nehemiah Chapter 8 illustrates their commitment to teach others.

The reading of the law of God by Ezra, in Nehemiah 8, happens shortly after the finishing of the wall of Jerusalem. The leaders asked him to read them the book of the law so that everyone could see and hear. They built a great platform on which he could stand. The audience included all the people, men, women and children.

As people listened, they recognized that they had broken the Word of God and felt guilty. However, Ezra wanted them to see God's law as an occasion of gratitude and joy. The people promised to obey.

Ezra instructed them to celebrate the Feast of Tabernacles (Leviticus 23:33-43). This is the feast that was characterized by joy. The Israelites recounted God's provision during their journey from Egypt to the Promised Land.

ADAPTATION

Modern cults and sects attempt to discredit, add to, or misrepresent the teachings of the Bible. Some school teachers have teachings and ideas that contradict Christian beliefs. It is therefore very important that students know what the Bible teaches us, and it should not to be seen only as one more book.

When you teach this lesson, emphasize that the Bible is the Word of God, and therefore, its content is true. In it, God tells us the right way to live.

Many of your students have their own Bible, but have no ability to read. Encourage your students to ask their parents or an adult to read them Bible stories. And if someone wants to give a book to them, suggest to them that it be Christian. (Suggest some that you know and understand that they are Biblical.) Tell them to pay attention when the pastor or Sunday school teacher reads the Bible.

LESSON DEVELOPMENT

Introduction

Discouragement was present in Israel for a long time, and the possibilities for change were few. To build a city in these conditions in order to raise the mood was a difficult task. But God worked again with people who were willing to trust and obey. The people were not only encouraged, but also did the task in record time.

The next step was to help the people know the law of God. This would be a very spiritual wall, more important and necessary than a city wall, because it would help reject the erroneous teachings.

DEVELOPMENT OF THE BIBLE STORY

Emphasize how hard it was for the people to rebuild the walls, because they had none of the machinery that now exists. However, they did so with the help of God. After the important work, God gave them the most important job of all: to know the Word of God; and to know it, the people must decide to do it.

Emphasize that God's people not only listened to him, but also obeyed his word. If you can, take several sizes of Bibles or any type of parchment, in order to exemplify how the Bible was in the time of Ezra.

Remind them that the teaching of all the lessons of this unit has been the same: "trust and obedience." And that each of the people mentioned in the Biblical stories both men and women were always willing to believe and to trust in God's promises.

Take a paper or cardboard heart (preferably red) and enter the text of Psalm 119: 9 and 11 in it, one on each side. You can use these verses as you teach the lesson.

APPLICATION TO DAILY LIFE

Knowing God's law was as important for the people of Israel as it is for us today. Often for children, all kinds of doubts attack them, and they need a spiritual wall around them to protect them. Explain that the Word of God will be that much needed wall in their life.

Encourage students to establish a discipline of reading in their life. Let them know what books of the Bible they can start reading (the Gospels are recommended). Invite the pastor to visit the class to be the finale of the unit. This may be a good opportunity for him to recommend a book to them. Allow space so that there is a time of questions. (It is better if the pastor is with you, or someone he assigns.) Let students ask something related to the class, the unit, or any concerns or questions they have.

Be prepared. Your students can ask simple or very complicated questions. If you think you don't have sufficient Biblical knowledge, forget this recommendation. But make every effort to take it into account. If you don't know an answer, be honest and say you will find out.

ACTIVITIES

Ezra Reads the Word of God

You will need two worksheets for the students, scissors and crayons.

Give each student their worksheets and follow the instructions on it. After they have made their pyramids, ask them to place them on a table and ask the question: "How can I hear the voice of God to obey it?" (Let the children tell what is happening in the figures of the pyramid.)

Read Psalm 119:11. This passage tells us to keep the Word of God. Ask, "Where do we keep the Word of God?" (In our hearts.) Use the time while the children are making their pyramids to review the lesson and give them ideas of how to apply the lesson personally.

MEMORIZATION

This is the last lesson of the unit. Bring all materials used for the memory verse from all the lessons in this unit: heart, words and other things that you have made. Put them on the wall for your students to see.

Ask what they remember about each lesson; review the lessons with them using each of the options you used for the unit. If you can, bring some kind of reward for those students who have learned the verse for this unit.

CONCLUSION

Help students not to forget everything they need to take home. Thank everyone for attending today's class. If you consider it appropriate, allow some to take home some of the teaching materials you used during the unit.

Create anticipation for the next lesson, tell them it is the start of a new unit. Tell them the topic to make a connection and awakening interest in them for not missing.

Conclude with a prayer. (You can make a circle with your students and ask for volunteers to pray.) Thank God for Moses, Joshua, Hannah and Samuel. Pray for their students. Do not forget to ask for prayer requests and to include them in your closing prayer.

NOTES:

YEAR 1 UNIT V

GOD IS THE CREATOR

Biblical Basis: Genesis 1:1-10, 14-19, 11-13, 20-31; 2:7; Psalms 139:13-16; 104:24-30.

Unit Theme Verse: "*In the beginning God created the heavens and the earth*" (Genesis 1:1).

PURPOSE OF THIS UNIT

This unit will help your students:

- ✘ To know that God is the creator and sustainer of the universe.
- ✘ To know that people are God's best creation.
- ✘ To know that God has given humans the responsibility to care for creation.
- ✘ To know about the wisdom, power and greatness of God.
- ✘ To increase their sense of personal value and overall sense of security.
- ✘ Praise God for His wisdom, power, greatness and creation.
- ✘ Identify some ways we can care for God's creation, and convey this to others.

UNIT LESSONS

Lesson 23: God Created the Heavens and the Earth

Lesson 24: God Created the Plants and Animals

Lesson 25: God Created People

Lesson 26: God Takes Care of His World

Lesson 27: God Asks Us to Take Care of His World

WHY WE NEED TO TEACH THIS UNIT

The book of Genesis is the foundation for understanding the rest of the Bible. At school, or maybe at home, students have been exposed to theories that contradict God's creation. As you teach these lessons, do not try to refute other theories. Emphasize that the Bible says that God created the universe and everything in it that exists. We do not know exactly how he did it, but we believe that the Bible is true.

Children have a natural curiosity to know everything: where it comes from and how it works. Impress on them the demonstrations of power, as you see in the cartoons, from magazines or television. Build on these interests, to guide the students to have a new appreciation for the greatness and power of God, the Creator. Help them understand that these stories are true and not imaginary fantasies.

God does what no one else can do. The knowledge that he is in control of this world should help your students develop a sense of security and confidence.

LESSON 23

GOD CREATED THE HEAVENS AND THE EARTH

GENERAL ASPECTS

Biblical Basis: Genesis 1:1-10, 14-19

Memory Verse: *"In the beginning God created the heavens and the earth"* (Genesis 1:1).

Lesson Objective: To help students know and recognize that God made all that exists in the universe.

TEACHER'S PREPARATION

In chapter 1 of Genesis, we find the word "God" 30 times. This shows that it was he who founded the universe and everything there is.

The creation is narrated in this book, and it should be read as a revelation of the nature and character of God the Creator. The Tyndale Bible Commentary notes that the expression: "God said," eliminates the possibility of a pre-existing universe. God consciously transformed the chaos and put it in to order, what was empty was filled with life.

The words: "In the beginning" describe what the book of Genesis is all about. Everything we see in our world today began through the creative power of God. Genesis is our basis for understanding the rest of the Bible, because it talks about the relationship between God and nature, between God and man and between men.

Genesis 1:2 describes the earth without form and void. But God began the creation of the universe by only expressing his will for it to be, that is, by his word. First he shaped the world; then he filled it with creation. Once he had finished, he was satisfied with what he had done.

ADAPTATION

Students always want to know the why. They often believe everything adults tell them. These two features make this an ideal place to teach that God is the one who did everything in the universe.

Students are developing a concept of God, and need to understand that he is more powerful than any other being in the world, and that he does what no one else can do. Help your students discover the power of the Lord through watching the way he reveals his creation.

Children still have difficulty with the concepts and relationships between time, space and distance. Explain creation using simple terms and give them the opportunity to ask questions.

It would be helpful if you find out what they have learned in school regarding creation. To do this, talk to some of the teachers or parents. Prepare your lesson regarding what students already know about the topic. For example, they know that the earth is round and consists of land and water. Also, we have night and day and the seasons. And at this age, they should already know the names of the days and months.

LESSON DEVELOPMENT

Introduction

The security that the students should have about the creation of this world and themselves is very important. They have already been exposed to ideas contrary to Biblical teachings-the different theories on evolution might have appeared in their life, so this is a critical stage. You as a teacher have a great responsibility to make the connection between Biblical truth and the students.

Pray to God for wisdom, and prepare the lessons well. Do not underestimate your students; They are no longer children who believe all of what they hear. Possibly, they will ask you profound and difficult questions to answer.

DEVELOPMENT OF THE BIBLE STORY

Take to class some element of creation that is small (a grain of sand, beans, rice, etc.). Then, introduce it to the students, and tell them that with all the modern technology, man is not capable of creating or making something as small as what you have brought them. Explain that what man can do is transform what was already created. (If you brought sand, tell them that with this and cement you can build a building; if you brought grains, that with this you can make different kinds of food.)

Emphasize that God's creation is not transformation; God didn't take something that already existed, he created it, he made it from nothing, only with the power of His word; God said it and it was done. Do not go into details; limit yourself to say they were days (for some are stages), since the concept of "one day" they understand better.

Emphasize the order and purpose of each of the forms God created. God did not do something by chance, or without knowing or having a purpose for it. On the contrary, everything he created has an order or purpose.

Explain to them that before creating the plants, trees and vegetation, God first made what they would need, such as air, sun and water. You can take photos where they can see the sun, moon, stars, the sea (where neither plants nor animals appear). You can use calendars from other years or magazine photos. Show the children the pictures and use them as support material for this lesson. Save the photos or place them on a wall. (If you want you can split the wall board into different days of creation.) Under each day put the name of what God created and some pictures to illustrate.

Remember to include songs with rhythm and movement, preferably before telling the Bible lesson. Thus, your students have already spent energy and will be ready to sit still for a moment and listen to the Bible lesson.

Look for songs that relate to the lesson. If you cannot find them then use chorus that speak of God's power. If it is possible, find cassettes or CDs of music for children, or get songs online.

APPLICATION TO DAILY LIFE

Make sure that students understand the concept of creation (evolution or transformation). It is important to learn about the origin of what exists; it will be a strong foundation in their faith. They must understand that all creation, including ourselves, are God's creation; and that he, in his wisdom and power, has created all that still remains to this day. This speaks to us not only of a creator God but also a sustainer.

It's important for your students to understand that the same power and love is available to each of them. This should give them a sense of security and a solid foundation for their Christian faith.

ACTIVITIES

God Created the Seasons

You will need a worksheet for each student, scissors, glue, crayons. Each student will need to cut out the pictures of children dressed according to different seasons and the names of the seasons, which is found in the CUTOUT section of the student book. Then give each student the worksheet that goes with this lesson. Help them glue the pictures of the children in the correct season picture, and then glue the season names below the corresponding picture of that season. Talk about how everything God has created works together. God is so wise and powerful that he made the sun and the moon to work together, and also the different seasons. Let students discuss what they know about the seasons. Give them time to color their worksheets.

God Created

Give everyone a worksheet; read the instructions and be sure that everyone understand what to do. Then let you students do the word search. Help them if they need help.

MEMORIZATION

If you chose to place photos of each day of creation on a wall, a blackboard or elsewhere, you can put the memory verse underneath the pictures. If you do, place it somewhere where your students can see it. Try to make it large.

Draw a picture of something in creation or take a picture (include all you can). Be creative. If you use pictures, don't cut them in square shapes, but cut them out and stick them next to the verse. If you have a computer, type the verse in large letters; then cut out each letter and glue them on cardboard.

Place the verse where it can easily been seen and leave it for future classes. Repeat the verse with your students several times. Perhaps it will seem like a lot of work, but remember that children learn best with visual aids.

CONCLUSION

Help your students not to forget what to take home. Thank everyone for attending today's class. Give them a hit about what the next lesson will be, trying to make a connection and creating interest so they won't want to miss it.

Conclude with a prayer. Do not forget to thank God for his creation. Ask if they have prayer requests and include them in the final prayer.

LESSON 24

GOD CREATED PLANTS AND ANIMALS

GENERAL ASPECTS

Biblical Basis: Genesis 1:11-13, 20-25

Memory Verse: *"In the beginning God created the heavens and the earth"* (Genesis 1:1).

Lesson Objective: To teach students to be thankful for God's marvelous creation of animals and plants.

TEACHER'S PREPARATION

Last week, we learned how the universe was formed. Evidence of order in God's creation is one of the wonders of the process.

Plants cannot grow without light or water, so God first created these elements rather than vegetation. Plants are a necessary food source for animals and humans, so God created them before creating animals (Genesis 1: 11-13).

To ensure the continuity of the process that he had begun, he created the system so that through the seeds, this will continue again and again. He also created the creatures of the heavens and the sea (vv. 21-31). Reference winged animals not only materializes in birds, but refers to everything that flies, including insects. In verse 22 we see that God blesses the creation with beings from the skies and seas; He tells them to be fruitful and multiply.

He also ordered that the land produce living creatures, each according to their species or genus. Genesis 1:12, 21 and 25 tells us that God was pleased with the plants and animals he created.

ADAPTATION

Children are naturally curious. They are in the age of questions. Many already know something about plants and animals. They understand how plants grow and have seeds. They also know that animals live in different places (water, sky, mountains, deserts, etc.), and also that they protect themselves.

What they already know becomes the basis for strengthening the Biblical truth that God created plants and animals (domestic, wild, birds, insects, reptiles and fish). It will not be long until your students are in conflict with the theories related to creation; this will only bring them confusion. Make sure your students understand that God is the creator of all that exists.

LESSON DEVELOPMENT

Introduction

We recommend you have a time of prayer specific for the needs of the students. Ask God for wisdom to sow the truths of this lesson in their hearts. You can start the study with songs related to the lesson teaching, preferably ones that have movements.

DEVELOPMENT OF THE BIBLE STORY

If in the previous lesson you used the division of creation days, start the class talking about the creation on different days. For this lesson again bring photos or drawings related to the lesson (including forests, flowers, animals, insects, etc.). Then, place them on the corresponding day.

If you did not follow the division of days, we recommend you do it for this lesson. Place the subject of the lesson in big letters, then put the pictures under the title of the lesson. Again, emphasize the order and purpose of God in creation. This will make your students aware that God is a God of order and purpose.

Before creating the animals, God created everything they needed to exist; thus we see an order and a purpose for each of created things. God did not create something whimsical or disorderly. On the contrary, creation shows us an artist who paid attention to even the smallest of details.

Find out in advance about the wonders of creation; of how the universe is so well formed, so that it has remained without being destroyed over the centuries. You can emphasize the fact that the earth revolves around the sun and the moon around the earth; and that our position in the universe is planned. If we were closer to the sun, it would burn us, and if we were further away from it, we would freeze.

APPLICATION TO DAILY LIFE

Your students are in a transition stage, so it is important to understand the concepts and Biblical truths of creation.

If you can, bring natural or plastic flowers to better illustrate the lesson. Give one to each student to take home. Tell them that this will help them remember this lesson, and to tell their family and friends.

It is important to understand the great love of God behind creation, because the Lord did everything for us. Make sure they understand these truths well. Give them time to ask what they did not understand.

ACTIVITIES

Plants and Animals Help Us

You will need a worksheet for each of the students, and crayons.

Let your students put the pictures in order of how things happen by placing numbers in the boxes provided. Make sure to use common sense and help them.

First row: small cow (1.)big cow (2.)Milk (3.)

Second row: Plant in the pot (1.)Plant in the ground (2.) Plant in vase. (3.)

Third row: Puppy with child (1.) Dog alone (2.) Dog with puppies (3.)

Fourth row: Plant in the pot (1.) Plant in the ground (2.) Fruits in the basket (3.)

This activity is intended to help your students understand that from the beginning, God created everything with a set order, process and purpose.

God is the Creator

You will need a worksheet for each student and pens or pencils.

Give each student the worksheet, and tell them to try to discover the secret or hidden message. This activity is designed to spark interest in your students. Remember that they like to discover; to know the reason why.

Encourage them to decipher the hidden message. Tell them to see if they can decipher aspects of the Creator, God Himself.

Have them complete the worksheet by writing at the bottom the names of 2 plants and 2 animals that they would like to thank God for.

MEMORIZATION

Requires a sheet of paper for each student, crayons, scissors and glue.

Print the memory verse on a sheet of paper (one for each student). If you can, use a font that is hollow in the middle, so that students color the letters. Give each student their sheet of paper and let them color it. Ask them to write their name on the back. (If they need help with their name, you can write it for them.)

Then have them draw a picture of something that they have learned about creation. (You can bring small cutout flowers and animals for them to paste on their pictures.) Repeat the verse together. If your students want to, allow them to take their picture home; or if they don't want to take them home, place them around the big verse that you made.

CONCLUSION

You can finish the class with a song that involves movement. If you want, you can include this game: draw or put on the floor a symbol (maybe an X). Then have the children sing and walk around the room passing over the signal. While the children are walking around, stop the song; the student who is standing on the symbol when the song stops gets to say the name of an animal or plant whose first letter is the same as the student's name. (For example: Ronaldo could say, radish or rat.) Continue the game until all or most of your students have participated.

Help your students remember what to take home (worksheets, etc.). Thank everyone for attending today's class. Give them a hint about the next class to build anticipation, trying to make a connection and create interest in the next lesson so they won't want to miss it.

Conclude with a prayer; Do not forget to thank God for his creation (including names). Ask the children if they have prayer requests and include them. If you were playing with them, you can ask the last one on the signal to say a little prayer and then you finish. (If the child cannot or will not, ask a volunteer to do so.)

NOTES:

LESSON 25

GOD CREATED PEOPLE

GENERAL ASPECTS

Biblical Basis: Genesis 1:26-31; 2-7, 19-24; Psalm 139:13-16

Memory Verse: *"In the beginning God created the heavens and the earth"* (Genesis 1:1).

Lesson Objective: To teach students to value themselves so they'll have good self-esteem; and to express gratitude to God for having created us in his image and likeness.

TEACHER'S PREPARATION

Both the creation of light and animals demonstrates the power and wisdom of God. What God created in the initial stage was a basis for what was to come later ... man.

Man was the climax of creation; only us did he make in the image and likeness of God. Although we are related to other creatures he formed, only we have God as Father. We are like a reflection of him in the world. God is the original model, with which human beings should be compared, if you want to know the true nature of man.

Eunice Bryant highlights the implications of being created in the image of God and says: "The Bible clearly defines the human being as a rational and moral being. We have a conscience and personal determination. We are different from the rest of creation, by the fact that we have a direct connection with the spiritual world. We know of the existence of God and we can communicate with him. And through the Bible and the Holy Spirit, the Lord communicates with us."

Only people have the ability and are equipped for the special task that God has entrusted them: to govern nature. Because we were created in the image of the Lord, we have the ability to worship, love, obey, trust and be faithful to our Creator.

Of all the creatures God made, only humans can develop and maintain a personal relationship with him. And therefore, we have the privilege and responsibility to work with the Lord.

Psalm 139 describes how God wants to be close to us. He wants to have a personal relationship with humans at very deep levels. He wants to have intimacy with us, but he already knows us intimately because he made us. He formed us from the womb of our mother; knows us like we were woven or formed; provides our days and knows our thoughts.

ADAPTATION

How was the universe formed? It is not a difficult way of thinking for most children; the knowledge that God made the world and everything in it is sufficient and satisfying. The important thing to stress is that God is the Creator. This is fundamental to correctly understand him and his creation.

It is important to understand that although man is classified within the category of animal, human beings are very distinct and different from other animals created, because we were the highest creation by God.

Each person is important and has a special value to God. These are the Biblical basis for proper self-esteem and to understand what are our skills and what should be our attitude toward possessions. You as a teacher can help your students to experience this personal truth; this can be achieved if you love them, value them, and accept each one of them.

LESSON DEVELOPMENT

Introduction

It is very likely that your students already have knowledge or theories of the evolution of man. One of the general ideas of this theory is that we have evolved, we have not been created. Another belief is that we descended from some animal, some suppose a monkey; others say some fish. If students have been exposed to this type of information, it is important to highlight the fact that we are God's creation, and made in his image and likeness.

DEVELOPMENT OF THE BIBLE STORY

You can start the lesson with a action song like "Jesus Loves Me" or another song that talks about creation. If you are doing the division of days on the lessons, remember to bring pictures of people. Try to include all possible races, men and women; and all ages. It is a good idea to bring pictures of people at different stages of life and show them to your students. Put them in the assigned place.

During the lesson, highlight the Biblical truth about the creation of man. Start by asking about previous lessons. Say, "How do you think we were formed?" "Where did people come from?" (Allow students to respond.) Use this as a base to know what points you need to emphasis. At the end of the lesson, review with your students, asking questions to make sure that they got the message.

APPLICATION TO DAILY LIFE

Your students are naturally curious. When they see people from different cultures, they want to know where they come from. Use this curiosity to highlight the fact that all of us descended from the same creation: God made us. And although there are many different cultures, skin colors, eye colors, sizes and shapes, we are all God's creation and he loves us all, even though we speak different languages and have different customs.

ACTIVITIES

God's Special Creation

Give each student a worksheet and let them decide which of the statements are true and which are false. (The first two are false and the last two true.) They can draw sad faces for false and happy faces for true. Discuss any questions with your students. Then allow them to complete the verse at that bottom of the worksheet by drawing a line from the correct word to the blank space where it belongs.

Different, But the Same

Read with the children Psalms 139:13-16 and allow them to complete the worksheet. Tell them that God made each of us special, and that every person in the world is important to the Lord. He knows us even before we're born. Ask the questions on the worksheet to continue your discussion.

1. How are these children the same? How are they different: (Accept suggestions from students regarding similarities or differences, such as: all are human beings, we all have feelings, some are boys, others are girls, one has a disability, etc.)
2. Which of these children were created by God? (All of them.)
3. Who does God love the most? (He loves them all the same.)
4. Who do you think God wants you to show love to? (All of them.)

My Friend and I

Give your students time to fill in the information asked for in this activity. If anyone does not know how to write, help them fill in the blanks.

MEMORIZATION

For today, bring the memory verse written on different pieces of paper that have been cut into different shapes of clothing/laundry. (One word of the verse on each piece. The pieces can be things like a shirt, pants, socks, towels, sheets, etc. Use large pieces for big words and small for small words. You could also use actually clothing and pin the words to the clothes.) In class, place a string across the room like a clothesline. Then, using clothespins, put each word of the verse on the clothesline. Have the children repeat the verse. Then, begin to remove some of the words and say it all again. Repeat until you have finished the entire verse.

When you have finished, save all the words and use them for the next class. If you want them to last longer, wrap the pieces with clear adhesive plastic. You can also color them, write the words by hand or glue them. If using a computer, make sure they are big enough to be seen from far away.

CONCLUSION

Help your students remember what to take home (worksheets, etc.). Thank everyone for attending today's class; give them a hint about the next lesson to build anticipation for the next lesson so they won't want to miss it. Close with prayer. Do not forget to thank God for creating people in his image and likeness.

NOTES:

LESSON 26
GOD TAKES CARE OF HIS WORLD
GENERAL ASPECTS

Biblical Basis: Genesis 1 and 2; Psalms 104:24-30

Memory Verse: *"In the beginning God created the heavens and the earth"* (Genesis 1:1).

Lesson Objective: To help students develop a feeling of security and know that God is in control of the universe.

TEACHER'S PREPARATION

God not only created, but he also provided what is necessary so that everything could continue to function. When he separated the light from the darkness, creating day and night, he started the cycle of 24 hours for each day. The sunlight in the morning and every drop of rain reminds us that he is in control of his creation.

By creating plants and animals also, he gave them the ability to continue to reproduce while maintaining their own kind. Every plant and animal born assure us that the Lord continues to control the universe and not only gives us life. When he formed Adam and Eve, he told them to multiply, to fill the earth.

Psalm 104 is a hymn of praise to God, Creator and Sustainer of our world. In the song, the psalmist includes a stanza (vv 27-30) talking about how God sustains life on earth. Verse 30 declares that his creative power continues until today.

Knowing that our God, who made the universe many years ago, is the same that continues to sustain it, should give us a sense of security and confidence.

ADAPTATION

Children usually don't value what they see every day, such as sunlight, vegetation, animals, and mountains in places where there are. They have the concept that the world is well formed. However, they are already at an old enough age to start thinking about who did all this.

The past three weeks you taught the students how the earth was formed. Those lessons were important to develop a suitable concept of God. But it is important that they know what the Lord's plans are for this world going forward.

It is likely that your students have already learned a lot about life and the planet, such as food chains and life cycles. Let them discuss what they know about it. Based on what they already know, you help them discover ways God uses to keep creating. That will give them a sense of security.

God gave each living creature the ability to reproduce so that their species or genus continue. If students ask you how people have children and animals, tell them to talk to their parents or relatives about it. If you want, offer to help by providing Biblical material containing information about that. They can also ask the pastor to help advise them.

LESSON DEVELOPMENT
Introduction

Everything that depends on man can fail, such as electricity, drinking water, gas, gasoline, etc. And although we may have sufficient money for these services, if they fail we cannot use them. Have you thought about what would happen if the same thing happened with God? What if man was in charge of supporting creation? Can you imagine if those who were responsible for scheduling the days go on strike, and instead of having day and night, we had three nights together, without days? Or the water ended, or we weren't able to burn or the sun melted. It would be a terrible mess. It is important to recognize that it is God who is in control of everything and not man.

Think of a river that you and your students know. Mention that it is possible that our grandparents swam in this place, now you do; and it is possible that in the future their children will as well. But this river has running water 24 hours a day, day after day. The water does not end, and we can be sure that it never will end because it is under God's control. That tells us about his faithfulness.

Remember that you can use other examples in this lesson.

DEVELOPMENT OF THE BIBLE STORY

Be sure to include songs that speak of faithfulness of God in sustaining his creation. Emphasize that he didn't just make the creation and forget about it, as does the mankind in many of his works, but on the contrary, the Lord sustains it.

The Bible teaches us that God established the limits of the sea. It's been many years (centuries); there have been many generations and the creation remains. Call the attention of the children to the photos they have seen during this unit. Highlight the fact that God has taken care of his creation: the flowers are growing, the seasons never fail to happen correctly, the sun always rises, the air is still available, water is flowing, and life goes on. This teaching will help your students to realize how false the theories are of the evolution of coincidences. The order of creation and subsistence of it speaks clearly of a God of order and power. Seeing a world so well formed, it is ridiculous to think that is the result of an accident.

It is as ridiculous as thinking that a clock is formed by itself. Seeing the perfection with which it is made, anyone can realize that there was someone who made it. The same applies to creation. It is impossible to have formed one by chance. Someone had to have done it, and that someone is God.

APPLICATION TO DAILY LIFE

Knowing that God cares for his creation should provoke in learners a sense of security and confidence. Take this opportunity to say that, in the same way that God cares for his creation, he wants to take care of our lives.

ACTIVITIES

God Cares for the World

Give the worksheet to your students as well as pencils, colored pencils or crayons, and markers.

Read the instructions and work with them on the first two sentences. Allow children to fill in the spaces with the corresponding answers. Then read the answers they have found, which are: sun, rain, seeds, babies, food, family, and friends. Use this activity to support this lesson: God cares and takes care of creation.

God Thinks of Everything

Ask, "What would creation be like if we didn't have God's help to look after it?" (Let children think about it for a moment. Some of them may have difficulty thinking of an answer.) Ask, "What if the sun didn't come every day, or what if it didn't rain? What if farmers didn't know what they would harvest when planting their seeds or if a pregnant woman didn't know whether she would have a baby or a giraffe?"

Children must understand that there would be chaos in this world. Let them propose other types of problems we would face if God did not care for this world the way he does.

Have them look up in their Bibles Genesis 8:22 and read it together. Then, ask how they feel knowing that God takes care of creation (Give them time to give some answers. They could be: We have security, trust, we are happy, etc.)

Allow your students to color the picture on their worksheet and to write a prayer of Thanks to God at the bottom.

MEMORIZATION

Use the clothing or cutouts with the words of the verse on them that you used last Sunday. Put up the clothesline again. Put it near where the large text has been pasted on the wall to guide the children. Put the pieces in a disorderly manner in a basket or other object. Then ask for some volunteers to come forward, take a piece and hang it on the clothesline using clothespins. Let others also participate until they hang the entire verse. When they have finished, say the verse together. When you're done, save the verse to use in the final lesson of this unit.

CONCLUSION

Help your students remember what they should take home (worksheets, etc.). Thank everyone for attending today's class; create some excitement about the next lesson, trying to make a connection and create interest so they won't miss the next lesson.

Finish with a prayer. Do not forget to thank God, not only for creating the universe, but also for taking care of it. Thank the Lord for taking care of the life of each of the students in the same way that he has looked after nature. Ask the children if they have prayer requests and include their requests.

NOTES:

LESSON 27

GOD ASKS US TO TAKE CARE OF HIS WORLD

GENERAL ASPECTS

Biblical Basis: Genesis 1:26-30; 2:15, 19-20

Memory Verse: *"In the beginning God created the heavens and the earth"* (Genesis 1:1).

Lesson Objective: To teach students that they can participate in the care of our world.

TEACHER'S PREPARATION

After God created Adam and Eve, he put them in the garden of Eden, which had everything they needed. And although the Lord could care for his creation alone, he wanted people to work with him. The first job assigned mankind was to work the land. The first job that is mentioned in the Bible is agriculture.

God also gave Adam the responsibility to care for the animals. His first task was to name each one. That job gave him the opportunity to discover the intellectual capacity that the Lord had given him.

ADAPTATION

God has given humans the responsibility of caring for the world he created. Children already know this. School, television and other media warn us about the need to protect our natural resources. However, they do not connect those resources with God as the creator and sustainer of all.

Emphasize the fact that every time they help in some way to care for or preserve nature, actually they are obeying God. Use examples from your city or country that show how people do to care for natural resources the Lord has left us.

Plan a project with students outside the classroom. In this way they can put into practice what they have learned. Those can be: planting flowers, trees, work in the church or in the neighborhood, etc. Take the opportunity to reinforce what they have learned.

LESSON DEVELOPMENT

Introduction

If you have used photographs to develop the previous lessons, you can also do it for this lesson. Take some where people are caring for nature (watering plants, cleaning, picking up trash, etc.). You can also use photo clippings from newspapers or magazines. Glue them around the ones you have already placed. Focus your students' attention on the fact that natural resources have a direct relationship with God, since he is not only the creator of them but also the maintainer.

Explain that people in the photos, whether they know it or not, are doing the will of God and obeying it in order to accomplish the task he set out for humans: care for creation. If desired, you can include photos of actions that go against to care of nature (littering in the street, oil in rivers and seas, mountains destroyed, etc.). Tell them that this is not pleasing to God.

DEVELOPMENT OF THE BIBLE STORY

Emphasize that man was not created to lie down and rest all day. It is likely that your students have this impression of Adam and Eve. Some believe that in paradise they only had to reach out and the food was ready. Even in the drawings that are made of paradise you never see Adam and Eve working. Incredibly, that has a negative psychological effect on children. Some even come to assume that work is a punishment from God for man's disobedience.

The Bible tells us that God had Adam till the land and look after it (Genesis 2:15). It is important for your students to establish the relationship between the care of nature and work. The fact that Adam would call them animals shows us the great responsibility that God placed upon him. Man is the climax of the creation of the Lord and has the responsibility to care for nature.

This lesson may include songs that speak of our responsibility to work for creation. It may be the one that says: "Oh, if we all work together, united," or some other similar song. Be sure to include movements in songs. Ask the children to form pairs and put them face to face holding hands. While singing, together they move their arms forward and backward.

APPLICATION TO DAILY LIFE

Children should be aware that the care of nature is something that concerns us all. It is very likely that most of them only have a vague idea as to our responsibility to maintain God's creation. Perhaps they think they are too small for that, or that it is something adults should do.

Use this lesson to inform them that, as children of God and obedient to His Word, this responsibility is also for them. First, make sure they understand that creation and God are connected to each other; God is the creator and sustainer, but he hopes that human beings do their part in preserving this planet.

Emphasize that they must be responsible for this. Ask about what ways they think they can help. (Some answers may be: depositing the waste in its place, not destroying plants or trees, not wasting water, etc.) Ask again how can we worsen the situation. (Some answers are: littering in parks, cutting the flowers for no reason, throwing garbage into rivers or seas, killing animals for pleasure,etc.)

ACTIVITIES

God is the Creator

Give the worksheet to your students, as well as crayons and markers. If you want to and if it's available, you can also use watercolors.

Give each student their worksheet and tell them to draw what the worksheet is asking for in each square; sky, animals, plants, and people. If children are using watercolors, be extra careful so that the children don't get their clothes dirty.

While students work, ask which of the things created by God is their favorite. Remind them what Psalms 104:24 says, and emphasize the wisdom of God.

I Can Help

Read with the children the instructions on the worksheet. Then, allow them to play the game. They can do this in pairs so that everyone can participate. Explain the instructions carefully and play with them so that they understand.

MEMORIZATION

Using the clothes with the words of the verse on them that you used in the past couple of lessons. Hide the clothes in the classroom. You can tape them under a chair, behind a drawing, or elsewhere. When it's time for memorization, ask the children to help you locate the text that is lost around the room. When someone finds a piece, they can go hang the clothes they found on the clothesline using clothespins.

As the pieces are placed in order, repeat the verse with the students. When they have finished, repeat it again. You can use this kind of visual aid to explain the importance of God's creation. For example, you can say that before man designed the dryer, people used the sun to dry clothes, and in many places people still hang their clothes outside to dry. It takes the sun and the air to dry the clothes. Mention that it is very important that the air is clean, because otherwise the clothes can become dirty. For example, if the air is contaminated with smoke from a factory, or if someone has lit a fire near where clothing is, this will make the clothes dirty and smelly from the smoke.

Use this to emphasize the importance of human participation in keeping the environment clean from pollution.

Another element necessary for cleaning clothes is water, and this must also be clean. In some places water travels through a pipe to the house so people can use it, some people get their water from a well, but in many cases people must go to a river or stream to wash themselves and their clothes. Whichever way we get out water, it is God who provides it.

CONCLUSION

Help your students remember the things they need to take home (worksheets, etc.). Thank everyone for attending today's class. Tell them that this was the last lesson of the unit, that you will be starting another unit next Sunday. Try to get them interested so they won't want to miss. If you think you can, give them the photos you used during the lessons. If you placed some of their work on the wall, let them take it home. You can also give someone the verse or save it.

Finish by singing and praying with them. Remember to thank God for creation, for taking care of it and for trusting that we will help care for it. Do not forget to ask if they have requests; if there are any, include them.

We recommend keeping record of all the prayer requests. At the end of the unit mention them all, and thank God for those that received a positive answer.

YEAR 1 UNIT VI

THREE SPECIAL FRIENDS OF JESUS

Biblical Basis: Luke 5:1-11; 3:21-22; 7:18-23; 8:40-42, 49-56; 9:28-36; Mark 10:35-45; John 21:1-17

Unit Theme Verse: *"You are my friends if you do what I command"* (John 15:14).

PURPOSE OF THIS UNIT

This unit will help your students:

- ✗ Know what it means to "Follow Jesus".
- ✗ Understand why Christians believe that Jesus is the Son of God.
- ✗ Be sensitive to discovering the importance of loving others and following Jesus Christ.
- ✗ To decide to be followers of Jesus, as the Holy Spirit guides them.
- ✗ Seek God's help to love and serve others as Jesus did.

UNIT LESSONS:

Lesson 28: Jesus' Friends Follow Him

Lesson 29: Jesus' Friends Know Who He Is

Lesson 30: Jesus Teaches His Friends

Lesson 31: Jesus Shows Love to His Friends

WHY WE NEED TO TEACH THIS UNIT

Your students have a broad sense of friendship; maybe some already have a group of friends who are becoming an influential factor when they are making decisions.

There are some popular sayings that say, "Tell me who your friends are and I'll tell you who you are."; or "A rotten apple rots others." And although it seems a bit radical, the friendships that children choose can influence their behavior now and may even define much of their future.

This is one reason why your students need to study this unit, so they can learn how to choose their friends.

Explain to them that we don't get to decide everything, such as: what family we're born into, who our neighbors will be, or who our classmates at school will be.

It is very important for them to understand that they can decide who their friends will be. This unit will help your students value good friendships; but, above all, to understand that Jesus wants to be and should be your best friend. We can have a personal relationship with him because he is not far from us.

Another important thing to teach children is that they can serve others. Some of these lessons will help them begin to identify with other people and to look for ways that they can help them.

We learn to serve others by example or by following a leader. When students see their Sunday school teacher, their parents, the pastor and other Christian leaders serving others, they will understand better how they can do the same.

Put in the hearts of children the desire to want to be like the one who is the Best Leader: Jesus Christ.

LESSON 28

JESUS' FRIENDS FOLLOW HIM

GENERAL ASPECTS

Biblical Basis: Luke 5:1-11

Memory Verse: *"You are my friends if you do what I command"* (John 15:14).

Lesson Objective: To help students understand what it means to follow Jesus.

TEACHER'S PREPARATION

This passage speaks of two pairs of brothers who were fishermen. They used to fish in the Sea of Galilee.

One day while Jesus taught people by the sea, and so many were pushing toward him toward the water, Jesus asked Simon if he could use his boat to teach from.

Jesus was no stranger to the fishermen, or a stranger to asking to use the boat; he was a friend to them.

When he finished preaching, he told Simon to do something that seemed crazy. They had tried all night to catch some fish without success. When the Lord asked him to use his boat, Simon had already washed his nets after finishing a hard night's work.

At the end of preaching, Jesus asked the fisherman to go offshore to deep water and throw out their nets. Simon explained that they had been trying all night to no avail. But he was obedient, and did what he was told.

What happened next humiliated the expert fishermen in front of a carpenter. The nets were filled with so many fish that they began to break. James and John came to help; it so filled both their boats with fish that they were in danger of sinking by being overweight.

Simon Peter recognized the power of God in the miracle of the miraculous catch and fell to his knees in the presence of the Lord. After witnessing this miracle, the two pairs of brothers, Simon Peter and Andrew, and James and John, did not need more persuasion to stop fishing and follow Jesus.

ADAPTATION

People follow their leader. Leaders whom the students choose have a lot of influence on their development. Help them to see Jesus as a leader who they can follow without fear, and to trust that he will not make them make bad decisions.

Remember that you as a teacher are the leader of the students; therefore give them an example of what it is to love and obey God. Do not forget that children think literally. If you tell them to follow Jesus, they can understand literally and wonder how it is possible to do that.

Explain that following Jesus means to voluntarily choose to obey his teachings.

LESSON DEVELOPMENT

Introduction

This lesson is an excellent opportunity to teach students what it means to "follow Jesus". The miraculous catch contains some concepts that your students do not know. One is that in those days, the nets that are used for fishing were very different from today. Currently the nets are often plastic. Although it is a thin material, it is resistant and transparent.

In Biblical times, the nets were made with a thick cord, so they only fished at night; if they did during the day, fish would see the net really well and it would be hard to catch anything.

Another element is the fact that the fish came close to the shore to find food; so Jesus' command to go deep and throw nets at that time of day with the sun shining seemed illogical. However, Simon obeyed saying, "I will do as you command". In other Bible versions it says: "In your name." Use these aspects as a framework for your story.

DEVELOPMENT OF THE BIBLE STORY

Tell the story creatively. If you can, bring a fishing net, hooks, twine or fishing photos. If you have them at your fingertips, bring some of the things used by fishermen such as an oar, a miniature boat, a lifeguard, etc.

Emphasize the following points of the lesson:

- ✘ Jesus was not an unknown person to the fishermen. Perhaps he was a friend, because Simon obeyed without saying anything. (We know that this fisherman was strong-willed, and if he did not know Jesus, he would not have obeyed.)

- ✘ Jesus' instructions were not logical, however, Simon obeyed.
- ✘ Seeing the miracle, these men were willing to leave everything (including the fish they had caught) to follow Jesus.

Include active songs that relate to the lesson. Remember to use your time well (including texts, songs, crafts, activities, etc.). Try to keep the same schedule throughout the unit. If you can, plan that in advance. This will help you be more effective.

APPLICATION TO DAILY LIFE

Tell students that following Jesus is to obey His Word; It is not like following someone on the street. On the contrary, it is an act of internal willingness to obey God's Word.

Your students are imitators and always follow a leader or friend. Highlight the fact that the best leader and friend of all is Jesus. He never leaves us nor is wrong. We can approach his presence with confidence, knowing that he understands us and is willing to work miracles in our lives. What we do is what they did. Simon Peter, Andrew, James and John were willing to follow, although that represented leaving behind everything.

ACTIVITIES

Who is Following Jesus?

Give children the worksheet, crayons, markers and pencils. Ask, "What do you think Jesus meant when he told the fishermen to follow him?" (Give them time to answer.) Highlight the fact that following someone can have different meanings. One way to follow someone is to do the sames things that the person you are following does, to want to imitate everything they do.

Use the worksheet to show the different meanings of the word "follow". Play the game "Follow the Leader" with the children. To play "Follow the Leader" you are the leader. Line the children up behind you and march around the room; the children must follow you. As you march, make movements with your hands; the children must imitate what you do (like clapping, raising your hands, putting your arms at you sides, shaking your arms and hands, crouching down, jumping up, etc.).

Then invite a student to be the leader and you go behind them. After some time, deliberately stop following the leader's actions and do something different from what the leader does. Some kids will do what you do instead of imitating the leader. When this happens, ask them how it makes them feel and discuss what happened. Say, "When I was the leader, all (or most) of you followed me and did the same things I did. But when (say the child's name) was the leader and I was behind them and did not follow their movements, I was not obedient."

Give students the worksheet and say, "When Jesus lived on this earth, his friends could follow him in two ways. What was one of them?" (They could follow him from one place to another.) "But his early followers also followed him in another way. How did they follow Jesus?" (They obeyed his teachings, followed his example.) "Did all people on the worksheet follow Jesus in this way?" Have the children take turns reading the written statements of each of the followers, and let them decide who followed Jesus' teachings.

Then ask them to color the clothes of the people that followed Jesus' teachings. (They should color those who say, "I believe in him," "I am going to do what he says," "Listen to him, he's telling the truth," and "I like what he says".)

Ask, "Can we follow Jesus from one place to another as Peter, Andrew, James and John did?" (No, because he is no longer in physical form like he was with them.) "So how can we follow him?" (By believing in him, knowing his Word, following his example and obeying his commands.) Repeat John 15:14 with the children.

What Will They Do?

Say, "Peter, Andrew, James and John left their work as fishermen to follow Jesus from one place to another; they learned to follow his example and obey his teachings."

"Children today must decide what Jesus would like them to do in every difficult situation. For example, let's look at the situation that appears on today's worksheet." Follow the instructions on the worksheet.

Define what is happening in the top picture (a girl dropped her tray and food splattered on some of the children, some children are upset, others are laughing). Ask students to write what they think the children are thinking. (Opinions can be varied. Ask why they think that.) Say, "Do you think that this is what Jesus wants us to do? Why or why not?" In the bottom picture, have the children write what a follower of Jesus would do (help the girl collect her belongings and clean up, speak kindly and encourage others to be nice to her.).

Mention that it is not always easy to follow Jesus; sometimes we are not sure what we should do. Sometimes we don't want to be different from our friends for fear that they will be angry with us.

Some students may not want to admit that they have

failed to be followers of Jesus. Discuss some experience in which you failed and did not act as a follower of Jesus. This will help students to know that, in the classroom, we can be honest.

MEMORIZATION

Draw the shape of a big foot and write the memory verse in the middle of it. Tell your students that the shape of a foot represents the footprints left in the sand as you walk through it, and this will remind us that we are following Jesus. You can do several feet and put one word of the verse on each shape. Then, place the footprints on the wall of the classroom. (The size of the footprints can be that of a sheet of paper.) Repeat the verse with your students several times.

CONCLUSION

Help your students remember what to take home (worksheets, etc.). Thank everyone for attending class today and give them a hint about the next lesson by telling them the title, creating a sense of excitement so that they won't want to miss it.

Conclude with a prayer; ask if they have requests and pray for them.

NOTES:

LESSON 29

JESUS' FRIENDS KNOW WHO HE IS

GENERAL ASPECTS

Biblical Basis: Luke 3:21-22; 7:18-23; 8:40-42, 49-56; 9:28-36

Memory Verse: *"You are my friends if you do what I command"* (John 15:14).

Lesson Objective: To help students know that Jesus is the Son of God, and he can do what nobody else can do.

TEACHER'S PREPARATION

The four passages of Luke in today's lesson show us the credentials of Jesus. God proclaimed that Jesus was his son, Jesus showed his power with a series of miracles, and when he was baptized, the Father's voice was heard from heaven identifying him as His son.

Jesus' ministry was probably not all that John expected from the Messiah. John sent two of his followers (disciples) to ask him if he was the Messiah or if they should wait for another. Jesus didn't answer with a simple yes or no; He gave evidence that he was the Messiah.

John's disciples saw for themselves that Jesus did what no one else could do. He never used miracles to prove that he was the Messiah. His miracles were fulfillments of prophecy. Sight to the blind and freeing the captives was the fulfillment of the messianic role described in Isaiah 35:56. Preaching the gospel to the poor fulfilled the prophecy of Isaiah 61:1.

Luke 8:40-42, 49-56 This story begins with Jairo's plea for his daughter. Again, Jesus showed that he could do what no one else did. While others were doubting and mocking, Jesus invited the parents of the girl and his close friends (Peter, James and John) to witness the miracle of the resurrection of the child, giving more evidence that he was the Son of God.

Luke 9: 28-36 - In the Transfiguration we see again close friends of Jesus as witnesses of an important event. They heard a voice from heaven proclaiming Jesus as the Son of God. They were sad that they did not understand fully the significance of what they had just seen.

ADAPTATION

Jesus is very different from all men. He is the only one who can proclaim that he is the only begotten Son of God. His miracles provide evidence of his relationship with the Father. This lesson will help your students understand this relationship. Knowing that Jesus is the Son of God will help you better understand who he is.

LESSON DEVELOPMENT

Introduction

It is very important to know people. When someone wants to have a position in a company, the first thing that their managers want to know is who is the person applying for employment. If in your house someone is needed to look after the children, your parents will want to know who that person is. If we are going to establish a friendship with someone, it is important to know who they are.

Similarly, if we develop a friendship with Jesus and we want to trust him with our future, we must know who he is.

Children are very trusting, sometimes they are willing to follow or obey anyone even without knowing them. Therefore, it is important to awaken their curiosity to find out who the people are. Tell them that in this lesson we will learn who Jesus is.

DEVELOPMENT OF THE BIBLE STORY

Over the years, people have had different opinions about Jesus. Who was he? For some, he was a good teacher, for others a great preacher, for others a phony. It is important to highlight the following points of the lesson:

1. **Jesus is the son of God.**
2. **Jesus is the Messiah.**
3. **Jesus is our Friend.**

Remember to use songs related to the lesson. The rhythms give the incentive of movement to children. For example: "Jesus loves me", "I have a friend who loves me", "His name is Jesus," etc. Emphasize that as friends of Jesus, we must know who is he to tell other children about him.

APPLICATION TO DAILY LIFE

Ask several students about the relationship they have with their best friends. Ask them to name their names, where they live, what they like to do with them, what they do not like about them, etc. Use this little dialogue to highlight the fact that we know about our friends.

Likewise, your students should try to have information about Jesus if they claim to be friends with him. Emphasize that Jesus is the Son of God and also our friend. This is a good lesson to tell those who do not know Jesus that they also are able to know him today, and get to have a personal relationship with him.

If they do, lead the children in this important step. (You can review the material of the last unit: "After a child is saved," which will be very useful.)

ACTIVITIES

Who Is Jesus?

Give each student a worksheet, as well as crayons and markers. Direct their attention to the reporter and the television camera. Tell them that these people are doing an interview and looking for the answer to an important question: "Who is Jesus?" Ask your students, "Why do you think that this question is important?" (Point to each person in the illustration and read their response. If your students believe the answer is correct, they should color in that speech bubble. Have your students place a star next to the best answer. All answers, with the exception of, "I do not know", are partly true, but the best answer is "the Son of God".)

Jesus Shows That He is the Son of God

You will need scissors and brass clasps for each student. Find the cutouts in the CUTOUT section that are needed to complete the worksheet.

These pictures remind us of the signs by which we know that Jesus is the Son of God. Have students follow instructions and help them to insert the pieces so that the dove descends from heaven onto Jesus. Ask volunteers to tell each of the stories that appear in the pictures. These stories serve as evidence to let us know that Jesus is the Son of God.

Ask the following questions:

- ✘ What did the voice from heaven (God) say when Jesus was baptized, and when he ascended to heaven? (This is my son.)
- ✘ Why is this statement important? (Because it leaves no doubt that Jesus is the only begotten Son of God.)
- ✘ Why do you think it was important that Jesus did these miracles? (To fulfill the prophecies.)

MEMORIZATION

Bring the memory verse written on a footprint (like the one used in last weeks lesson, but smaller, so that each student can have one.) If you can and have the resources, make them sturdier by putting clear adhesive plastic on them. Make them small enough that they can be used as a key chain. Tell the children to put their name on the back before laminating them. Then make a hole in the heel of the foot. You can place them on a ring or a piece of yarn. Encourage your students to put it in a place that they will see it and be reminded of the verse (i.e. the zipper pull on their backpacks, on the door of their closet or bedroom, or hang it on the mirror that they use every morning to get ready for school).

Repeat the verse with them several times. Then ask what it means to them. (Allow them to answer and explain their answers, as many times your students don't have the words to answer completely.) Ask if they believe that Jesus has ever asked them to do something bad or wrong.

CONCLUSION

Help your students remember the things that need to be taken home (worksheets, crafts, etc.). Thank everyone for attending today's class; create some excitement about the next lesson, trying to make a connection and anticipation so they won't want to miss it.

If there is time, sing a song that has motions. Also review the lesson by asking questions related to Jesus; and see how much attention the students paid to the lesson. Conclude with a prayer. Do not forget to thank God for having sent Jesus to be our friend.

NOTES:

LESSON 30

JESUS TEACHES HIS FRIENDS

GENERAL ASPECTS

Biblical Basis: Mark 10:35-45

Memory Verse: *"You are my friends if you do what I command"* (John 15:14).

Lesson Objective: To teach students to recognize the greatness of serving others.

TEACHER'S PREPARATION

In the two preceding chapters (8 and 9), it mentions that Jesus tried to prepare His disciples about the problems that would arise around Him. However, they were blinded and concerned about their position, and did not realize the imminent danger that was coming.

James and John were still thinking that the kingdom of Jesus would be earthly. They did not want to lose the opportunity to have positions of power. It is incredible that shortly after the second warning of Jesus concerning the approaching trial (Mark 9:31), they were still trying to get a position of power in the coming kingdom of God.

Jesus denied the request to sit on his left and his right because they failed to understand the magnitude of this request. In the Beacon Bible commentary, Dr. Ralph Earle describes the request of James and John as follows: "While Jesus was thinking of a cross, they were thinking of crowns. His responsibility was met with their blindness; His sacrifice with their ego. He just wanted to give, they to get. His motivation was service, theirs was personal satisfaction."

Jealousy and unwholesome ambitions lead people to act as foolish and wayward children to get what they want. Jesus does not describe true greatness in terms of position and authority, but of service. His words were concrete when he said he was the Son of God. He came to serve humanity, even the most insignificant of human beings.

ADAPTATION

Although children are already more sensitive to the needs of others, they still have a lot of self-centeredness, which is a quality of children smaller than them. They can be very aware of what bothered them, but what they do that annoys others is often unnoticed.

It is still very difficult for them to see the perspective of others. Yet, Jesus says that greatness is based on service to others. This service requires some skill to make us realize the needs of those around us.

This lesson will help your students start to identify with others and seek ways in which they can serve. Following the example of others is a key method for student learning.

The first lesson of this unit talks about following Jesus. Serving others is also learned by example or following a servant leader. When newcomers see their Sunday School teacher, their parents, the pastor, and other Christian leaders serving others, they will understand better how they too can serve.

LESSON DEVELOPMENT

Introduction

Children have little ability to serve others. For them, criticism and mockery is more common than helping each other. In this lesson, you have the opportunity to lay a solid foundation that will help develop Christian character of service in the lives of your students.

Pray that God will help you teach this lesson and make sure the students understand it. We recommend that you help them think of ways that they can serve others, such as helping another child do a task that they do not understand, either in church or school, help their mother around the house picking up toys; putting trash in place, etc.

Emphasize the difference between human and spiritual values; we often value things and people only from the human point of view. We think, "follow what has value". However, if we consider spiritual values, everything changes. The value of people has to do with service to others.

DEVELOPMENT OF THE BIBLE STORY

Start by asking, What makes a person important? (If necessary, briefly express what you are referring to.) Allow time for students to answer.

Continue with the questions: How many of you would like to be important and why? (Let the children answer.) Using their responses as a parameter, tell them that today's lesson is exactly that, "How to become someone important in life." If you can, bring photos of important people (presidents, kings, movie stars, politicians, etc.).

Explain that in the eyes of the world, these people are important, but why? (Let them respond.)

Then tell them that if we ask these people what makes a person important, their answers could be varied. "I want to introduce you to the most important person in the history of mankind. Indeed, his birth divided history, so that the years are counted retroactively before his birth, and then progressive after him. Do you know to whom I am referring?" (Give them time to respond.)

Answer, "Yes, his name is Jesus." Place a picture of Jesus' face above the other photos that you brought. If you did not bring any, you can put titles on some papers, noting the name of Jesus on another and put his above all others. Then ask the children to pay close attention. Tell them that this lesson about Jesus will tell us how to become the most important.

Now narrate the Biblical history. Try to be creative. You can change the tone of voice when needed. Try to speak differently when it comes to another person. Do your best to not read (master the passage to avoid mistakes). Move, walk from one place to another and make movements, as if you were the character who is speaking, so that the children live the lesson.

APPLICATION TO DAILY LIFE

It is important that your students understand that as followers of Jesus, they are to live a life of service. This is not a nice concept for them, especially the fact that for most of their life, they have been treated and served. As you know, customs often become law, and at this age, sometimes it's hard to understand these concepts because they have to leave their comfort zone and risk rejection.

ACTIVITIES

Searching for Kind People

Give students the worksheet for today's lesson plus the searchlight from the CUTOUT section of their activity book. They will also need scissors and metal clasps/brads.

Have them put the searchlight in the center of the worksheet, and then rotate it to focus on the four different situations on the worksheet. Allow volunteers to tell the class what they think is happening in the illustrations.

Ask, "Are the people in the illustrations important? Why or why not?" Encourage your students to participate and talk about what they see in each situation, and what makes them think that the people are important.

Explain, "When you do not know a person, you might think that person is important if you see that they have a luxury car, a big house, fancy jewelery, expensive clothes, etc. In the Bible story today, Jesus talks about true greatness."

If You Want to be Important

Give your students the worksheet with two wheels on it and ask them to cut out the wheels. The wheel that has the figure of Jesus goes on top, the one that has the phrases goes underneath. Also, cut the circles inside the speech bubbles to display the words on the bottom wheel. Then put a clasp/brad in the middle of the wheels so they can turn. Show the children how you can turn the wheel and see different messages in the bubbles. Take time to read the statements. Use this activity to review the points of the lesson.

Service Award

In the CUTOUT section of the student book, the student will find two awards. Ask the children to cut them out and paste them on cardboard. Then ask who did something special for someone else during the week. Ask them to tell the class what they did. For example: helped their mom wash the dishes, picked up their toys, etc. Pin a badge on the chest of children who helped someone during the week.

Card: Something Special for Someone Special!

Ask the children to think of two special people who are not their parents or siblings. Then ask them to cut out the cards from the CUTOUT section and let them give the cards to the special people they thought of. Ask them to tell the class why these people are special to them.

MEMORIZATION

Write the memory verse on the board (or bring it written on sheets of paper, placing one word on each sheet.)After you have written the verse (including the reference), ask your students to say it out loud. Invite a volunteer to come forward, erase or remove one of the words and repeat all the verse including the missing word. Then ask another volunteer to come forward and erase/remove another word. Continue until all the words are erased or removed. If you can, reward the students who have memorized the verse. Remember that children are motivated when there are rewards. If you wish, you can include the verse from the last unit as a form of review.

Emphasize the importance of learning Bible memory verses.

CONCLUSION

Help your students remember what to take home (worksheets, crafts, etc.). Thank everyone for attending today's class; get the children excited about the next lesson by trying to create interest and a desire to want to come again. You can sing a song with motions or review the lesson.

Do not forget to say a prayer before leaving the classroom. Doing this is very important because children learn not only to pray, but they see it as an essential part of life.

NOTES:

LESSON 31

JESUS SHOWS LOVE TO HIS FRIENDS

GENERAL ASPECTS

Biblical Basis: John 21:1-17

Memory Verse: *"You are my friends if you do what I command"* (John 15:14).

Lesson Objective: To teach students that Jesus Christ never stops loving us.

TEACHER'S PREPARATION

John chapter 21 shows Jesus' deep love for his disciples. It also shows how they responded to this love. At the beginning of the story, we see them returning from Galilee to go fishing. Most likely, they were seeking to escape the questioning and criticizing from the crowd in Jerusalem; or they returned because Jesus asked them to go to Galilea and wait for him there (Matthew 28:7).

Another reason could be because they were feeling discouraged about the death of their teacher. They felt confused and disappointed and they had decided to return to their previous profession—fishing. Whatever the reason may have been, their lives were in the middle of an emotional storm; their future seemed uncertain and they didn't know what to do.

Evidently, Peter still felt a huge amount of guilt for having denied Jesus. So the disciples returned to fishing in the same place where the teacher had found them and called them to follow him.

The miraculous catch in John 21:17 is parallel to the miraculous catch when Jesus called his disciples to follow him (Luke 5:4-7). On both occasions they had been fishing all night long without having caught anything (Luke 5:5; John 21:3), and on both occasions Jesus asked them to take their nets and try to fish one more time. Both times the nets were filled with fish.

The repetition of the similar miracles was a key for John, because he was able to recognize Jesus.

In verses 15-17, Jesus asked Peter the same question 3 times: "Do you love me?" He had also denied him 3 times. Now, by the fire prepared by the Lord that loved him, Peter had to affirm his love for Jesus 3 times.

ADAPTATION

The appropriate response given the love that God shows us through Christ is to love him too. Jesus' love for his disciples and for us isn't just an emotion. He showed them a love so strong that he could confront them when they did something wrong, and even stronger to forgive them. Jesus didn't give up on his disciples, even when they had failed him in the biggest test they had faced up to that point.

The students have also faced failure and they need to know that God will not give up on them. Just as Jesus loved, confronted, and forgave his disciples, in the same way he will not give up when it comes to us. This love and commitment from the Lord inspires us so that we also can love him and commit to him.

LESSON DEVELOPMENT

Introduction

The students are very conditional with their love. They will only show it to someone who they believe has earned it. But if that person does something to hurt them or something they don't like, they stop loving them. Because of this, this lesson will help them to understand the way Jesus loves us, with an unconditional love that does not depend on our way of loving him.

DEVELOPMENT OF THE BIBLE STORY

This Bible story emphasizes Jesus' love for his disciples; a love that did not give up when Peter denied him, nor when the disciples abandoned him. It explained the similarities between the miracles of the great catch when Jesus called his disciples and when he looked for them (lesson 28). He had called them to be fishers of men, yet here they are again fishing.

Point out the fact that Jesus did not get upset or scold them. Rather we see the opposite; we see in him a great tenderness and love for them. In preparing the fire for them where they could dry off and eat, we see a helpful, servant Jesus (lesson 30). Ask, "What would you do if you had told a group of your friends to do something, then returned to find out that they hadn't done it?" (Let the students respond.)

Explain to them that the way Jesus reacts is amazing. He showed love to his friends. Remember to include in your class songs that lend themselves to the topic. For this lesson, you could sing "Yes Jesus loves me, the Bible tells me so."

If you use this song, prepare some visuals like the silhouette of a large heart shape (preferably red). Inside the silhouette write the first phrase of the song "Jesus loves me".

Then make the silhouette of the Bible (can be open or closed) and inside write the next phrase of the song "the Bible tells me so". Ask 2 volunteers to hold up the visuals while you sing the song.

APPLICATION TO DAILY LIFE

What a great lesson the students can learn from today's story! They need to learn to forgive, be tolerant, be patient, and show love to the people who let them down, just like Jesus did. But what happens sometimes is the exact opposite. They are demanding, impatient, slow to forgive, and if they don't like someone, they simply put up a barrier between themselves and that person.

ACTIVITIES

Jesus Shows His Love

Give your students the worksheet, colored pencils, and markers. Ask them what objects are missing from the picture: the net full of fish, fish in the disciples' basket, fish on the fire Jesus is building, bread in the basket by Jesus. Give them time to draw all of the missing pieces.

Ask, "How does Jesus show his love for his disciples through the objects that you drew?" (Jesus came to look for the disciples, even when they had previously abandoned and denied him. He helped them fish and he prepared their breakfast. He was not mad at them, he forgave Peter for denying him.) "How did the disciples respond to the love Jesus showed them?" (They were happy to see him; Peter told Jesus three times that he loved him.)

John 21:16

For this activity you will need the small squares with pictures in them from the CUTOUT section that go with this lesson, the worksheet for today's lesson, scissors, and glue.

The verse on the worksheet comes from today's Bible story. Read the verse from your Bible and explain what it means. (Many times the Bible refers to people as sheep; Jesus told Peter to love and care for people just as a shepherd loves and cares for his sheep.) Have the children cutout the pictures and paste them onto the worksheet in the correct places; check that they do it correctly. When they have finished, repeat the verse together.

MEMORIZATION

Using the verse that you made at the beginning of the unit, review it with the children. Since this is the last lesson, make sure that all of them have learned it. If you have time, ask each child to repeat it.

If you think that one verse per unit is too easy for your students to learn, you can use 2 verses per unit, or one verse each week. If you do this, make sure that the verses are relevant to the lesson.

CONCLUSION

Remind the students to take their things home (worksheets, etc.). Thank each student for attending class today. Give a small recap of the unit. Give a preview of what is coming up in the next lesson, trying to make a connection and spark interest in the students so they do not miss class.

If you did the memory verse using the individual footprints (lesson 28) and you still have them in the room, give each student one to take home. The visual material that is left over can be used to reward students (for timeliness, attendance, good behavior, participation, etc.).

Finish with a prayer. Thank God for the marvelous friend we have in Jesus. Ask him to help the children follow him and recognize who he is. Ask Him to help them serve him and love others like Jesus loves.

NOTES:

YEAR 1 UNIT VII

GOD THE FATHER

Biblical Basis: Exodus 19; Leviticus 19:1-4; Hosea 1:1-2; 6:1-3; 14:1-2; Luke 15:11-24; John 14:1-27; Acts 2:1-4

Unit Theme Verse: *"You, Lord, are forgiving and good, abounding in love to all who call to you"* (Psalm 86:5).

PURPOSE OF THIS UNIT

This unit will help your students:

- ✘ To describe God, the Father.
- ✘ Know that God is faithful and holy; and that He treats us better than we deserve.
- ✘ Trust that God is faithful to keep all His promises because He loves us, even when we fail Him.
- ✘ Experience the love of God in their lives. That they will know to seek Him when they make a mistake to ask Him for forgiveness.
- ✘ Begin to understand that the Trinity is the unity of 3 people in 1 God.
- ✘ Know that God is always with them through His Holy Spirit.

UNIT LESSONS

Lesson 32: God is Holy

Lesson 33: God is Faithful

Lesson 34: God is Love

Lesson 35: God is Always With Us

WHY WE NEED TO TEACH THIS UNIT

Children almost always confuse God, Jesus, and the Holy Spirit; but it's not only them, many adults do too. The doctrine of the Trinity is important and essential in the lives of all Christians. God in 3 persons, but being only 1 God. This is a difficult concept to understand, but the church recognizes it as truth and a basis of the Christian faith.

This unit introduces students to the mystery of The Trinity by focusing their attention on God the Father. As was already mentioned, this is a difficult concept to explain and understand for a majority of Christians. Without a doubt, it is very important for the children to begin to understand how the Father, Jesus Christ, and the Holy Spirit are all related.

Knowing that God the Father is holy, faithful, and loving, and that he is always with us through the Holy Spirit who help us, should give us reassurance. This assurance will help to grow your students' love and faith in God.

Faithfulness is a quality that the students need to learn about God; even though they may already have an idea what this means.

Through the study of these lessons, the students will know that when they do not make good choices, they hurt God's heart and affect their relationship with him.

LESSON 32

GOD IS HOLY

GENERAL ASPECTS

Biblical Basis: Exodus 19; Leviticus 19:1-4

Memory Verse: *"You, Lord, are forgiving and good, abounding in love to all who call to you"* (Psalm 86:5).

Lesson Objective: To help students know that God is holy.

TEACHER'S PREPARATION

God is holy, and he calls us to be like him, holy. He wants a holy nation that honors him above all else. In Exodus 19, the Lord is preparing to establish a covenant with his people, as a holy nation, "You will be for me a kingdom of priests and a holy nation. These are the words you are to speak to the Israelites." (v. 6, NIV.)

To be holy means to be separate, set apart, to live lives that reflect the true nature of God. The essence of holiness, just as we find in the Bible, is that we be conformed to God's character.

On Mount Sinai, God made a covenant with the nation of Israel. God's part of the covenant was seen in the actions he took that were climaxed when he freed them from Egypt. Their part as his people was to give him total devotion and obedience of his commandments. The result would be a holy nation.

The cloud, the smoke, and the fire were visible signs of divine presence and protection. Israel responded to God by declaring, "We will do everything the Lord has said." (v. 8, NIV) They had the freedom to reject the Lord's proposition, but they chose to be obedient. God never obligates anyone to make a pact with him. What He does is create an atmosphere that motivates humans to give a positive answer.

The nation had gone through an intense preparation to be able to be with God at Mount Sinai. Their preparation took the form of an objective lesson which helped them to understand the purity of the Lord. All of the rules were in place to teach the nation about the necessity of holiness, total devotion and absolute obedience that God asked for.

God allowed them to have this experience to create in them a deep reverence for God and inspire them to completely obey his commandments.

Leviticus 19:1-4 - This passage is part of a longer section generally referred to as the Holiness Code.

This code gave instructions to the people for how to live a holy life in their daily lives. The word "holiness" is the key word in this book:

- God is the source of all holiness (vv. 1-2).
- God is the measure of holiness (v. 2).
- Holiness is separation from evil and unity with God (vv. 3-4).

ADAPTATION

This unit (God the Father) will help the students to begin to understand what God is like. In today's lesson they will learn about the holiness of God. This means that he is perfect, pure, without sin, and free from any kind of wickedness.

Dennis Kinlaw says, "Holiness should not be considered as just another characteristic or attribute of God. If you are going to see it as an attribute, it should be the attribute of all attributes. But in reality it is the essence of the character of God itself that determines the nature of his attributes. The holiness of God tells us about the difference that exists between him and his creation in terms of his importance, majesty, moral perfection, ethics, and sovereign love."

It is important to know that God is a God of holy love. This helps us to erase the common misconception that He is just waiting for us to mess up to punish us. Your students should not have the impression that it is impossible to please God. And they should know that he called his people to live holy lives.

To live a holy life is not an option that God presents to us to decide if we want to put it into practice. He gives us his grace so that we can be holy like he is holy. This is an exciting promise, not an irrational demand!

LESSON DEVELOPMENT

Introduction

It is important that the students develop the correct concept of God from an early age. For this reason it is necessary for them to understand the Lord's holiness. We cannot think about God the Father without connecting that to his holiness. This could be a new concept for some students; others may have heard about it before; perhaps others have misunderstandings of what holiness is.

This is why it is so important for you as the teacher to prepare especially for this topic. Remember that you are forging the way of the foundation of the spiritual lives of your students. Don't take this work lightly. You are not just teaching a Sunday school lesson, nor is the class meant to just entertain the children; you are shaping lives and preparing them for eternity! Take your work seriously; get on your knees and ask God to help you.

DEVELOPMENT OF THE BIBLE STORY

As you present the lesson, you need to be very careful about the vocabulary you use. There may be new students. Also remember that just because students have been attending church for a long time that does not mean that they have a good understanding of religious concepts/terminology. If you use words with symbolic or religious connotation, give a detailed explanation of their meaning.

Explain the concept of the Word 'holiness'. The students need to understand that this is the essence of God. It's not that God could be holy, or that he has the capacity to be holy, but that the Bible says: God is holy.

Explain to the students that holiness is not an option or an opportunity; it is a mandate ... a requirement. The Bible says, "Without holiness, no one will see the Lord."

Make the concept of holiness very clear. If you have doubts about the subject, don't hesitate to talk with your pastor. This is a concept that should become very clear to your students; one bad explanation or lack of clarity in your class could affect their way of understanding God. This is why it is so important that you prepare to present this topic very well.

Don't forget to include songs in today's lesson. If you wish, you could sing the hymn "Holy, Holy, Holy, Lord God Almighty" or any other song that relates to the lesson. Remember to include motions for the songs.

APPLICATION TO DAILY LIFE

Your students do not yet have a clear understanding of holiness and its implications. Tell them that this has to do with the way they behave in life ... that God is interested in a practical holiness, not a conceptual holiness. It isn't how much they know about holiness, rather how much of that knowledge they apply in their daily lives.

Explain to them that if God has asked us to be holy, it's because he has given us the capacity and made his help available to do so. Give some practical examples to go along with the teaching.

ACTIVITIES

Mystery Puzzle

Give your students the worksheet, scissors, and tape. If you are able to, also give them envelopes to put their puzzle pieces in. Give them time to cut out the puzzle pieces. Then they should choose the words that describe God and stick them together. When they have taped them together, have them turn the puzzle over and try to find the secret message.

Let them know that if they don't place the pieces correctly on the front, the message on the back will be hard to read. Say, "Because God is Holy, he wants us to be holy as well." Read the Bible passage from Leviticus 19:1-4. At the end say, "According to this Bible passage, what does God expect from holy people?" (That they respect their parents, that they respect the Sabbath, that they attend church to worship God, that they don't worship other gods, and that they love and obey God.) "What can you all do today to show that you honor and obey God?" (All of the above.)

Give your students an envelope to keep their puzzle pieces in. Tell them they can show it to their family or friends.

MEMORIZATION

For this lesson, you can cut out shapes to make a train. On the engine place the Bible reference, and on each car put one word of the verse (the engine and cars can be the size of a regular sheet of paper).

Once it is finished, put the train on the wall or chalkboard. (Do not glue it down because you need to be able to move it; stick the pieces up with a small folded piece of tape on the back of each piece.) Put the train in order and have the students repeat the verse. Then, turn over a few of the cars and have them repeat the whole verse (including the missing words). Repeat this until they are repeating the verse with all the cars turned over.

CONCLUSION

Remind the students to take their things home (worksheets, etc.). Thank each student for attending class today. Give a small recap of the lesson. Give a preview of what is coming up in the next lesson, trying to make a connection and spark interest in the students so they do not miss class.

Finish with a prayer. Ask the children to make a circle and hold hands. Ask them if they have any prayer requests and include the requests in your prayer.

LESSON 33

GOD IS FAITHFUL

GENERAL ASPECTS

Biblical Basis: Hosea 1:1-2; 3:1-2; 4:1-19; 6:1-3; 11:1-4; 14:1-2

Memory Verse: *"You, Lord, are forgiving and good, abounding in love to all who call to you"* (Psalm 86:5).

Lesson Objective: To teach students that God is faithful in all His promises because He loves us even when we are not faithful to Him.

TEACHER'S PREPARATION

To better understand the book of Hosea, we need to recognize the circumstances of the times.

Politically and economically, the nations of Israel and Judah were living in a time of prosperity. Both had very stable kingdoms and predicted an optimistic future.

Nevertheless, Israel found itself in a time of moral and spiritual failure. They had combined their worship of Baal with their worship of the true God. Their worship for the pagan idol (a Canaanite god) diluted their worship for Jehovah.

God used this moment to reveal Himself. This is the story of Hosea. Through him and his experience, we can see signs of God's love for mankind. This theology of love paves the way for the theology of love found in the New Testament.

Hosea is the first book of the minor prophets. The message to Israel, the pronounced vengeance of God on a weak and adulterous people, is tempered by the promise of God's mercy. This prophet denounces Israel's idolatry, predicts God's justice through captivity and deportation, and proclaims the end of captivity. He also talks about the total corruption of the nation.

God instructs Hosea to give Israel a modern example of love and faithfulness. He obeys the command and marries an adulterous woman.

As a future demonstration of love and faithfulness, God instructs Hosea to buy back his wife again (3:1-2). Obeying God would require not only a loving heart, but also a loving act. Hosea paid the price of a slave to get his wife back - this was redeeming love.

Hosea sets aside his personal tragedy to deal with the implications that this had for Israel as a nation (4:1-19). This prophet could see the fatal nature of the people's corruption, which is why he tried to persuade them to repent and be saved. He also announced that they would not escape their terrible fate.

The theme of the love of a father for his child is presented through the love of a husband for his wife. Hosea highlights God's love as a father calling his son (Israel), who had distanced themselves in favor of a false god, inviting them to come back to Him (11:1-4).

Hosea 6:1-3 and 14:1-2 - These two passages are a call to repentance. If the son who left returned repentant, God would forgive his sins and restore his position. This book has profound implications for our personal relationship with God. It challenges us to confront our own false gods and think of the judgment God will have for us for not fulfilling the pacts made on Mount Sinai and at Calvary through the blood of Christ.

Despite having received the incomparable love of God through His son Jesus Christ, we are often unfaithful disciples. We find it difficult to love those who hurt us. God is faithful and treats us better than we deserve.

ADAPTATION

What do your students know about "faithfulness"? Probably not very much. Defining this word is a key aspect of this lesson. Why is God faithful to humans? Because He loves them unconditionally and without merit. His love is so deep and strong that no one can understand it.

Help your students understand that God's love is constant, faithful, and unfailing. He treats us better than we deserve.

LESSON DEVELOPMENT

Introduction

Faithfulness is one of the qualities of God that children need to learn about, even if they may already have some concept of it. Some may have experienced it in some ways in their friendships.

DEVELOPMENT OF THE BIBLE STORY

Be sure that the students have fully understood the concept of faithfulness. It is probable that they have heard this word in different contexts; for example, it is sometimes used to talk about sound (high fidelity). Other times it is used to talk about spouses if both are faithful. Sometimes it is used to define interpersonal relationships, i.e. whether or not friends are faithful.

We recommend looking up the definition of faithfulness in various dictionaries, including a Biblical one. Be prepared to explain this quality, because just as holiness is born in God, He is the perfect and grand example of faithfulness in all of its expressions.

APPLICATION TO DAILY LIFE

Students need to learn that our response to God's faithfulness should be one of gratitude. Invite them to follow your example.

ACTIVITIES

What Do These People Deserve?

Give the worksheets to your students, along with construction paper and markers. Before class, write "faithful" on a piece of construction paper. On the back, write "God always fulfills his promises, even when people don't fulfill their promises to Him."

For this activity, allow students to describe what they see in each picture. Then allow them to say what the children in each picture deserve.

Ask, "Do they deserve to be punished?" The children may have different options about this. Help them come up with different possibilities for each situation. The picture with the children that have a bat may be tricky because they may not have been allowed to play in that location because they could break a window. The plane could have been broken on purpose.

Talk about the last picture (Jesus forgiving Peter after Peter denied Him three times).

Ask, "Did Peter deserve God's forgiveness?" (No, Jesus forgave him because He loved him and Peter had repented for what he had done.)

Ask, "If God is holy and does not accept sin, why doesn't He destroy people who sin?" (Allow them to respond.) Then show them the piece of paper with the word "faithful" written on it. Give the answer, "Because God is holy, He is also faithful." (Show the other side of the sheet.) Say, "God always fulfills His promises, even if we are unfaithful."

God Is Faithful

Ask, "What does this worksheet say about God?" (That He is faithful.) "How do we know He is faithful?" (Because the Bible gives us examples of His faithfulness.) Allow children to color in their worksheets. Help them to fold the ladder. Tell them that these are the steps that everyone (including themselves) must take to become children of God.

Explain that being a child of God is being a Christian and a follower of God; that it is belonging to His huge family and having the ability to love and forgive. Tell them that when we take each of these steps, we can be sure that God is faithful, that He forgives us, and that He welcomes us into His family.

MEMORIZATION

For this lesson make train cars like you did for the previous lesson, only smaller. Write the memory verse on each one and give one to each student. Then, using the larger train that you placed on the wall for last times lesson, repeat the verse together.

CONCLUSION

Before you end class, make sure your students do not forget what they need to take home.

For the final prayer, form a circle and join hands. Pray first and have your students repeat your prayer.

NOTES:

LESSON 34

GOD IS LOVE

GENERAL ASPECTS

Biblical Basis: Luke 15:11-24

Memory Verse: *"You, Lord, are forgiving and good, abounding in love to all who call to you"* (Psalm 86:5).

Lesson Objective: For students to experience the love of God in their lives, so that they know to seek God's Love when they make a mistake and ask for God's forgiveness.

TEACHER'S PREPARATION

Jesus told the story of the prodigal son during the last six or seven months of His life. He found Himself in Berea, on the east side of the Jordan. He was traveling to Jerusalem for the last time.

Some of the most beloved and best known stories of Jesus' life are found in the book of Luke (The rich man and Lazarus, the prodigal son, the good Samaritan, and that of Zacchaeus).

The first chapter contains three parables about loss: a sheep, a coin, and a son. The first two concern things of temporary value (the sheep and the coin); and the last with a person (the prodigal son.) But all are of eternal value.

Jesus contrasts the inclusive love of God with exclusive parables (so that not everyone would understand them). Jewish law dictated how a father should divide his inheritance. The eldest son should receive a double portion. It was uncommon to divide the inheritance before the father died , and even less common that the younger son should request it. (This was considered disrespectful to the father.)

In this parable, the younger son leaves home for a very distant country (possible beyond the border of Israel). The intense desperation in this young man is apparent in the fact that he accepts a job feeding pigs, the lowliest of jobs for a Jewish man.

The word "prodigal" refers to a person who squanders his property on useless things, without measure or reason. It can be compared to being "wasteful" or an irresponsible spender. In the story, the son was prodigal in the use of his inheritance.

When he returns to his father, the father gives him a robe, a sign of honor, usually given to a special guest. He also gave him a ring, which signaled authority, and shoes, which were a sign of the restoration of his position as son; slaves and servants did not use shoes.

Each detail is a symbol of the restoration of his previous position and his reacceptance as part of the family. Slaves were not part of the family. Employees and day laborers were contracted a day at a time and could be dismissed without notice. The prodigal son did not ask for the restoration of his previous position; he would have been satisfied with the precarious position of a day laborer.

"Dead" and "alive" are words with implications about the spiritual status of individuals, before and after a Christian conversion. "Lost" and "found" have implications of a search.

It was the love of his father that led this young man to take each step necessary to come home. This love was present as the son remembered his father, and the first idea he had was to go back. The love of God continues to seek out sinners today.

ADAPTATION

Students need to know that there is someone who loves them, regardless of what they do. They know when they do wrong. In this lesson, they will learn that when they act badly, they hurt God's heart and affect their relationship with Him. Because of this, they must repent and confess their sins to the Lord.

Jesus told this story to highlight the love of God and His concern with every part of our lives. Many students will have a loving father and can relate well to this parable. As a teacher, be alert and identify the students without father figures, and those who may have broken relationships with their fathers. In this lesson, highlight how our Heavenly Father is with us.

Students are afraid of being lost; many of them have been lost in one way or another. Or they may have been separated from their parents; those moments are scary for both parties. If they have never been lost, they will at least know the dangers associated with it.

Help them exchange the fear and pain of being lost for the joy that comes with being found, so that they can understand the love of God better.

LESSON DEVELOPMENT

Introduction

Students can tell when someone loves them. You as a teacher should show them love; if you do not, they will not want to be in your class. It is important that they begin to understand the spiritual implications of God's love.

The love of God demands a response. Throughout today's story, they will see how this love can cause us to make decisions and take action in response. Read John 3:16 to reinforce the theme of sacrificial love that God shows for mankind.

DEVELOPMENT OF THE BIBLE STORY

Do not forget to include songs in your class. For this lesson, you can sing "Jesus loves me." Consider substituting "Jesus" with "God." Remember that songs should include movements. If you want, you can write the song in a heart cutout with writing on both sides.

In today's lesson, emphasize the unconditional love of God. Remember there various types of love: "filial" (brotherly love for siblings and friends); "eros" (erotic or sexual love); and "agape" love (the love of God). John is known as "the beloved disciple." He says that God is love, not that He knows how to love or that He has the capacity to love, but John defines God as love.

The parable of the prodigal son is a clear example of the unconditional love of God, a love that expects nothing in return, that is not what we deserve, but though we do not deserve it, God continues to love us. He is holy, He is faithful, and He is love.

Help your students with a quick review of the characteristics of God that they have learned in this unit thus far. Allow them to explain in their own words what they have learned. This will help you to plan your next lesson, the last one in this unit. If you find a deficiency in any of these concepts, take note and prepare a review of the unit for the next lesson.

APPLICATION TO DAILY LIFE

Students must understand that the love of God is available to them. This lesson should also give them a sense of how dangerous it is to separate ourselves from the Lord, as the consequences can cost us our lives.

Emphasize the security that God's love provides us. Explain that God does not look at a person's age, but loves us all the same.

ACTIVITIES

The Loving Father

(Book to fold.) You will need the worksheets (4) for each student, scissors, and a stapler. (If you are making copies of the worksheets, be sure to copy the front and back on the same sheet of paper or glue the two copies together. If you don't, the book won't come out correctly.)

Make an example of the book before the lesson to learn the procedure and to serve as a helpful example for your students. Help them put their books together and make sure that the pages are in the right order before you staple them. (If you want, choose assistants to help your students; ensure that they know how to complete the task.) Use this book to review the Bible story. When finished, allow your students to take their books home to share with their family and friends.

MEMORIZATION

Using the train that you have used throughout the unit, remove it from the wall and hide the different train cars around the classroom or under the chairs/benches; you should do this before the students arrive.

When the time comes for scripture memory, call your students' attention to the fact that the train is missing; then, ask for help finding it. As pieces begin to appear, have each student who finds a train car stand at the front of the classroom with their piece. Then tell them to put the train in order. Repeat the verse multiple times.

CONCLUSION

Help students to remember what they need to take home (worksheets, etc.). Thank each student for their help. Briefly review the lesson, and give a preview of what is coming up in the next lesson, trying to make a connection and spark interest in the students so they do not miss class. Announce that the next class is the last lesson of this unit. Ask students to review what they have learned up until now.

End in prayer. Ask students to form a circle and join hands. Ask if they have any prayer requests and include them in you prayer.

NOTES:

LESSON 35

GOD IS ALWAYS WITH US

GENERAL ASPECTS

Biblical Basis: John 14:1-27; Acts 2:1-4

Memory Verse: *"You, Lord, are forgiving and good, abounding in love to all who call to you"* (Psalm 86:5).

Lesson Objective: To teach students that God is always with us through the Holy Spirit.

TEACHER'S PREPARATION

This passage is part of a series of lessons that took place after the Last Supper. This was the last opportunity Jesus would have to teach His eleven disciples. Judas had already abandoned the group after his treason.

Jesus had never spoken of this before; now His goal was to assure the eleven that He would always be with them by means of the Holy Spirit.

The word "counselor" is a legal term, but it has a defensive connotation, as in "a counselor to defend," which means "someone who is called." The Holy Spirit will always be with believers; its job is to guide us to truth and teach us all things. We also remember the words of Jesus when He said "I will be with you." This refers to two occurrences:

1. When he revealed Himself to His disciples (and other believers) after His resurrection.
2. His coming as the Holy Spirit on the day of Pentecost.

"Peace" or shalom was a common greeting between Hebrews, but Jesus uses it in this passage in an unusual way. The use of this expression refers to "salvation," to the redeeming work that would be done for all who believed in Him. A profound feeling of being spiritually well, based on the relationship we have with God.

The word "peace" in the Bible means "all that which contributes to our good." This does not mean the absence of problems or conflict. Regardless, nothing and no one in this life can take away the peace that Jesus gives us.

The day of Pentecost took place fifty days after the Sabbath or Easter week (Acts 2:1-4). The Old Testament refers to the day of Pentecost as the "celebration of the weeks" because there were seven weeks after the feast of the first fruits. The day of Pentecost is the most important event in the book of Acts. The Jews who did not live in Jerusalem traveled there for this celebration. For them, it was safer to travel by the Mediterranean Sea in the months of May or June (probable months of the feast) than to go in March or April.

When the Holy Spirit came, the disciples were all in the same place. The visible and audible signs of the wind and the fire marked its coming. Fire is the symbol of the presence of God, which fills the heart with purity and power.

ADAPTATION

Students often confuse God, Jesus, and the Holy Spirit. This is understandable as there are many adults who do this as well. The doctrine of the Trinity is essential to orthodox Christianity, but it is very commonly misunderstood. This lesson will help students know the difference. God is three persons while being one God; this is difficult to understand and explain, but the church recognizes this as true and fundamental to the Christian faith.

The good news is tied to the fact that God has not left us alone. When Jesus prepared His disciples for His departure He assured them that God would continue to be with them through the Holy Spirit. Pray to the Lord and help your students find the presence of the Holy Spirit, God with us.

LESSON DEVELOPMENT

Introduction

Students often have a well-developed sense of security. Take advantage of this to tell them that God assures us He will always be with us. He does this through the Holy Spirit, which is the fulfillment of the promise of Jesus to His disciples that He would be with them until the end of the age.

DEVELOPMENT OF THE BIBLE STORY

Prepare well for this lesson about the Holy Spirit, as students are sure to have lots of questions. We recommend studying the topic and referring any doubts or questions to your pastor. Begin the class by explaining what God's presence means to us today. Remember to include songs that allow children to move and that are related to the lesson. Some suggestions include "God is here," "Holy Spirit, Fill My Life," etc.

APPLICATION TO DAILY LIFE

The most important and relevant part of this lesson is that students have the security that God is always with us through the presence of the Holy Spirit in our lives.

ACTIVITIES

Three in One

Give each student a worksheet for this lesson. They have learned about God, and about Jesus when He was on earth. Today they will learn about the Holy Spirit and the ways in which he helps us. Explain that when we refer to God, Jesus, and the Holy Spirit, we refer to the Trinity (God in three persons.)

On the worksheet, students see how a person can be three in one. This one woman is a wife, mother, and grandmother all at once. Highlight this and allow students to list various roles that we can fill while being the same person (for example, they are sons, brothers, and cousins; yet, they are one person.)

Give them time to ask related questions. Be prepared to answer them.

The Holy Spirit, Our Helper

You will need four sheets of paper, 4 pieces of construction paper or cardboard, markers, four envelopes, and tape. Prepare the four squares in advance. Cut four squares out of the paper, making them all the same size. Write one of the four declarations (God, Father, Son, and Holy Spirit) on each square. Then, cut the squares into puzzles of five or six pieces and place them in envelopes (one envelope for each declaration).

Divide the class into four groups and give each group an envelope, a piece of construction paper and some tape. Then, ask them to put together the puzzle in their envelop and tape the secret message onto the construction paper. Use each one of the declarations to review the lesson. Explain each one of them. If you can, place their work on the walls for all to see. Allow children to color their sheets. Each declaration describes a fundamental function of the Holy Spirit in our lives.

Allow all students to participate by giving examples of each declaration in their own words.

Then, ask your students to complete the activity on the second page of lesson 35 (John 14:16).

MEMORIZATION

Place the train cars made for this unit in a basket. Ask each student (or those interested) to take one of the cars. Then, tell them to place them in order. You will take the engine with the scripture reference.

Then, have the students with train cars line up. Ask them to place themselves in order according to the verse. Have them walk around the classroom. You can do this while you sing a song. Have a parade. Say that the train needs fuel, or that they need to pick up passengers, or that they have arrived somewhere. Repeat the verse for each "stop" you make.

You can do this activity in small groups to see which one puts the verse in order the fastest. The important part is that you are sure that all the students have memorized the verse.

If you can, give a simple prize to those who memorized the verse. Remember that students are motivated when they are rewarded for something they do.

CONCLUSION

Help students remember what they should take home (worksheets, etc.). Thank each one for helping during class; give a brief review of the lesson and of the unit. Tell them something about the next unit that will peak their interest so that they will not miss class.

End the class in prayer. Ask the children to form a circle and join hands. Ask if they have any prayer requests and include them. If you wish, allow students to take home some of the materials used throughout the unit.

NOTES:

DAVID - FROM SHEPHERD TO KING

Biblical Basis: 1 Samuel 16:1-13; 17; 18:1-11; 19:1-10; 20:1-42; 24 y 26; 2 Samuel 9.

Unit Theme Verse: *"The Lord does not look at the things people look at. People look at the outward appearance, but the Lord looks at the heart"* (1 Samuel 16:7b).

PURPOSE OF THIS UNIT

This unit will help your students:

- ✘ Better understand what it looks like to fully trust God.
- ✘ Feel joyful in knowing that God values the love and obedience His people have for Him.
- ✘ Realize that trusting in God allows us to be more brave, faithful, merciful, and fruitful than we can imagine.
- ✘ Embrace the desire to follow David's example of trusting and obeying the Lord.
- ✘ Learn that God is powerful and the only one in whom we should place all of our trust.
- ✘ Have the desire to find friends who love and trust in God as they do.

UNIT LESSONS

Lesson 36: David is Anointed

Lesson 37: David Trusts in God

Lesson 38: David and Jonathan are Good Friends

Lesson 39: David Shows Mercy

Lesson 40: David Keeps His Promises

WHY WE NEED TO TEACH THIS UNIT

Students are greatly influenced by those around them. They try to imitate those they look up to. This is why it is important that they learn about "heroes of faith."

David is the ideal hero for preschool and elementary age children. His story begins when he was a little shepherd boy, the youngest of eight brothers. At his young age, he was confronted by a giant and he killed him. He developed a strong friendship with a prince and managed to escape an evil king. Later, he became a king, but did not forget his friendship with the prince. This may sound like a fairy tale or a legend, but it is a true story. Best of all, David trusted God.

These heroes are extraordinary. David was one of them. Your students could experience some of his greatness and know that they too can trust in God.

LESSON 36

DAVID IS ANOINTED

GENERAL ASPECTS

Biblical Basis: 1 Samuel 16:1-13

Memory Verse: *"The Lord does not look at the things people look at. People look at the outward appearance, but the Lord looks at the heart"* (1 Samuel 16:7b).

Lesson Objective: For students to understand that God does not value our appearance, but our love and obedience to Him.

TEACHER'S PREPARATION

When we scrutinize this first book of Samuel, we see how God rejected Saul as king of Israel, even when He had chosen Him some time before. God ordered Samuel to anoint a new king He had chosen, one of the eight sons of Jesse.

Samuel was afraid and aware of what would happen if Saul discovered there would be a new king anointed. The Lord directed him to fast and present a sacrifice during his visit to Bethlehem, as these priestly customs granted protection on the mission to which they were called.

Samuel evaluated each of Jesse's sons according to their appearance; the oldest was big and strong, which is why he thought that he was the one the Lord had chosen. But the Lord said to him, "Do not look on his appearance or on the height of his stature, because I have rejected him. For the Lord sees not as man sees: man looks on the outward appearance, but the Lord looks on the heart." After rejecting the first seven sons, Jesse called his eighth son who was caring for the sheep. Nobody would have expected the future king of Israel would come from a place as small as Bethlehem and that an insignificant shepherd would become the king of God's people.

When Samuel saw him, God said "Arise, anoint him, for this is he." And that was how Samuel anointed David as king of Israel in a ceremony used to designate priests, prophets, and kings. The popularity of the phrase "the Lord's anointed" reflects a divine initiative, which denotes an exclusive relationship between the God of Israel and the king who was named, to whom he gave power and authority to rule in His name. The king was God's representative on earth, who should be a faithful reflection of his character.

ADAPTATION

Very often, we, just as Samuel did, judge others according to their appearance and let our own opinions lead us. In the same way, children, though they are small, are very aware of the importance of appearances. Their hair and clothing can become the key to feeling accepted by society and their peers. God has a completely different view of human beings. He does not judge us by our social status, and much less by our physical appearance or intellectual capacity. He knows who we truly are.

In this stage of development, children begin to conform their appearance according to pressure exerted by their social context. We cannot prevent this from happening, but we can give them peace and strength, laying in their hearts the foundation of truth that God, who is superior to humanity, does not judge or value us according to our appearance. In this way, we teach them the precious value of the person on the inside.

LESSON DEVELOPMENT

Introduction: Vote for the King

Have the worksheets from the student book that corresponds with this lesson and a pencil for each child. Talk to them about how we choose leaders for games and what characteristics we look for. Ask them to tell you what they know about what people look for in a leader.

Read the instructions on the upper part of the activity, and give the children time to vote for a king. Ask for some volunteers to explain who they voted for and why.

DEVELOPMENT OF THE BIBLE STORY

Prepare in advance a crown and eight small signs with string attached to the top two corners so it can be hung around the neck of a child. Write a phrase on each sign like: the most beautiful, the most famous, the tallest, the thinnest, the smartest, the strongest, the best athlete, the purest heart.

Ask students who wish to participate to choose a sign and hang it around their necks. As you tell the story, walk past by each one, pretending that they are the sons of Jesse. Make sure that the student wearing the "purest heart" sign is last.

Tell them the story of how God choose a new king for his people. Draw attention to how God did this.

Ask "Would God have chosen the same king that we voted for?"

As you get to the part about the election of the new king of Israel, invite the students representing Jesse's sons to come to the front so that everyone can read their signs. Emphasize that each one is not exactly what God is looking for in a leader. Continue until you come to the last sign and put the crown on the child who represents David.

APPLICATION TO DAILY LIFE

To end the lesson, prepare a hand mirror, preferably a large one with a red heart attached to the back of it. Tell your students that you have brought a "magical mirror" to class that shows us what we see on one side and what God sees on the other side.

Allow each of your students to look into the mirror. As a child looks at themselves in the mirror, ask them to list some of the characteristics that they see in themselves, i.e. big eyes, long hair, etc. After each child has participated, invite them to see what God sees in each one of them and show them the side of the mirror with the heart. Ask "What does God see?" (Your heart.)

ACTIVITIES

What Do You See

You will need the student worksheet, scissors, envelopes, and markers. Follow the instructions on the worksheet to prepare for and play this game. (If you are making copies, be sure to copy both sides of the worksheet onto the sheets you give the children, or glue the two sheets together so that the cards have something written on the front and the back.)

To begin, each student will need their own cards to play alone or play with the group using one deck of cards and have your students take turns. It is likely that students will draw cards with different combinations. This affirms the truth that external appearances are not an accurate guide of what is on the inside of a person.

Explain to your students that it is difficult to know a person just by looking at them. A stranger can look very kind, but be very dangerous. Maybe some children do not have the prettiest toys or the best clothes. Regardless, they can be our best friends. It is good to know that God does not value us based on our external appearances, but on who we are on the inside.

A New King

Create or find two drawings of Samuel anointing David. Reinforce it with a piece of cardboard and cut it into puzzle pieces.

Divide the class into two groups. The object of the game is to complete the puzzle by correctly answering questions when it's their turn. Whoever answers a question correctly receives a puzzle piece. The first team to complete their puzzle wins.

If you prefer, don't use the puzzles and just ask the questions in a quiz competition between the two teams. Here are the questions:

- ✘ Who was the first king of Israel? (Saul)
- ✘ Was God happy with Saul? Why or why not? (No, because Saul did not love or serve God.)
- ✘ Who was Samuel? (A prophet of God)
- ✘ Who was king at this time? (Saul)
- ✘ Where did God tell Samuel he would find the new king? (In the house of Jesse in Bethlehem)
- ✘ What did God tell Samuel to do in Bethlehem? (Prepare a sacrifice and anoint the new king.)
- ✘ What did the city leaders ask Samuel when he came to their city? (If he came in peace.)
- ✘ How many sons did Jesse have? (Eight.)
- ✘ Who did Samuel think God was going to choose as king? (Eliab, Jesse's oldest son.)
- ✘ What did God tell Samuel about Eliab? (Do not look at his appearance, God looks at the heart.)
- ✘ What did God say about Jesse's older sons? (I have not chosen any of them.)
- ✘ Who did God choose as king, and what was his job? (David. He was a shepherd.)
- ✘ What is more important: external appearances or what is on the inside? (What is inside, the heart.)

Challenge for the Week: My Heart

Prepare a template of a heart (possibly out of construction paper) so that all students can make one. Distribute sheets of red paper or pieces of construction paper, pencils, and scissors to each child. Help them make a heart to take home as a reminder that:

- ✘ God knows our hearts;
- ✘ Appearance, toys, and clothes are not the most important parts of a person;
- ✘ We should try to have a clean and pure heart every day.

Ask students to write on their paper hearts all the good things that God sees in them.

MEMORIZATION

Discover the Verse

You will need the worksheets from the student book.

In class, help students to discover the memory verse with the help of the drawings. The illustrations will help them understand and remember the passage because they do not all know how to read or read well. Tell them that this verse is part of today's Bible story. This is what God revealed to the prophet Samuel about what he values in people.

Remind students that the word "man" in this verse does not only refer to adults, but to everyone.

CONCLUSION

Help your students finish any remaining work and tell them that they will learn the story of David throughout this unit. Encourage them to bring a friend to the next class and to tell their family about today's Bible lesson.

Ask if anyone has a prayer request, and ask a student to volunteer to pray and include those prayer requests.

NOTES:

LESSON 37

DAVID TRUSTS IN GOD

GENERAL ASPECTS

Biblical Basis: 1 Samuel 17

Memory Verse: *"The Lord does not look at the things people look at. People look at the outward appearance, but the Lord looks at the heart"* (1 Samuel 16:7b).

Lesson Objective: To teach students that God is powerful and He is the only one we should fully trust.

TEACHER'S PREPARATION

This chapter (1 Samuel 17) references a type of war that sometimes occurred in Biblical times. Despite the fact that armies were preparing to fight each other, each one chose an opponent for a duel that would determine victory for their people. The army of the winning competitor also won the battle, eliminating the need to fight each other.

When this happened, the Philistines had a very strong giant named Goliath as a warrior. He threatened and provoked Israel, daring them to send a warrior to confront him.

In ancestral cultures, for the most part, the king was the strongest. Popular leaders almost always became kings for the simple reason that they succeeded on the battlefield, or because they won a duel that led them to victory and freed them from a bloody battle.

King Saul was very important to Israel, as he was the tallest man in the country; many expected him to fight Goliath in Israel's name. But instead of accepting the challenge and fighting the giant, he offered his daughter, riches, and the cancellation of taxes to whoever would fight Goliath.

Many were tempted by this offer, but none were brave enough to face the giant as it would mean a certain death.

David had gone to the battlefield to complete a task his father had assigned him: to feed his brothers and make sure they were safe. While he was there, he heard that Goliath was challenging God's people and decided to confront him. Until then, no one had accepted the king's offer and David was the first to accept this challenge.

Saul met with David and, surprised by his weak appearance, rejected the possibility of sending him into battle, because if he lost, all of Israel would become slaves to the Philistines. But David, anointed by the power of God, convinced Saul, who finally accepted his offer.

Although the king offered his sword and royal armor, David was not prepared with any weaponry. His weapons were very simple in the eyes of the army: he had his faith and trust in God, his slingshot, and five smooth stones. Of all of them, his most powerful weapon was that all of his hope was in God, which he learned as a child. This is apparent in what he said to Saul, "The Lord who delivered me from the paw of the lion and from the paw of the bear will deliver me from the hand of this Philistine" (v. 37).

Young David was very aware that the battle was not his, but God's, as Goliath had not only challenged Israel but God himself, and he would be the one in charge of defending his people.

ADAPTATION

In this stage of development, students are faced with problems that we, as teachers, often ignore.

Depending on their social, familial, and economic status, their conflicts may vary, and are frequently generated by adults or different circumstances that they cannot control, such as divorce, separations, lack of protection and care, abuse, mistreatment, etc. These problems are usually the cause of psychological, emotional, and physical limitations which reveal themselves in shyness, attention deficits, rejection of expressions of love, fear of the dark, etc.

Maybe not all of your students face problems such as these, but they may have some minor circumstances that can affect their healthy development.

It is important that you as a teacher understand the personality and demeanor of each of your students to better meet their needs - spiritual, emotional, and even physical.

Through these lessons, children can strengthen their trust in God to find possible solutions to their problems. The conflicts in which they are involved can be too great for their level of comprehension. It is your task to guide them to focus on placing their faith and trust in God, knowing that He is the great one that all of their problems must face.

LESSON DEVELOPMENT

Introduction

Welcome your students and tell them to prepare to hear the story of a young boy who fought a giant. Ask them to imagine the size of a giant.

To help students understand Goliath's size, obtain a yardstick or measuring tape, three pieces of paper, tape, and markers.

With the help of measuring tape, measure 2.74 meters on the wall, and attach a piece of paper to the top that reads, "Goliath was this tall." If you wish, consider allowing children to lay down on the floor in a line and see how many of them fit within 2.74 meters. Then, measure an adult from your congregation and attach a piece of paper that says "many adults grow to be this tall."

Compare with your group Goliath's height to that of a normal person, and explain to them that the giant wore armor weighing more than 125 pounds, which is about the weight of two students. On the third piece of paper, write "Goliath weighed more than two of you combined." Place this piece of paper near where Goliath's chest would be.

When they finish the activity, seat your students and ask them how they would feel if a person of Goliath's size and strength were to fight them. Allow students to give their answers and tell them, "today we will discover what gave David the courage to fight this dangerous giant."

DEVELOPMENT OF THE BIBLE STORY

Give your students the worksheet entitled "David trusts in God" that corresponds to this lesson, and ask them "if you were to compare David's physical appearance with Goliath's, what would you say? (David was smaller, thinner, weaker, etc.) Based on physical appearance alone, who do you think would win the battle? (Goliath) Now they should pay close attention to the story to discover who won the battle and why.

You can use different ways to present this Bible Story. Use what you have, use some pictures or dolls to represent the Bible characters. If you do not have access to visual aids, we suggest that you use volunteers from your class to act out the story as you tell it. Bring in costumes, a toy sword, a fabric slingshot, etc. The important thing is that your students understand the lesson and can remember that they can conquer any problem when they trust in God.

APPLICATION TO DAILY LIFE

Give your students blank sheets of paper and pencils.

On the upper part of the paper, write, "God is more powerful than..." (Give them time to draw or write problems or fears that they may have that can be overcome by trusting in God.)

Establish a connection between your students and David, emphasizing that although they are small, they can face big challenges when God is by their side.

ACTIVITIES

David Trusts In God

Provide colored pencils to your students and tell them to write on their worksheet what makes Goliath strong and what makes David strong. If you wish, you can review the Bible story as your students work to reinforce learning and address questions or doubts. (If you make copies, let them color the picture.)

Trust In God

When they finish their picture of David and Goliath, your students should turn the page over to work on the next activity. They will need pencils and crayons.

Read together the affirmation that says "God is Bigger than any person or problem." Then ask your students to write their names on the line. In the blank space, they should draw something that shows them how to trust in God.

MEMORIZATION

Write the words of the memory verse on different note cards and hide them in the classroom. Tell the students to look for them and as they find them, they will need to put the words of the verse in order and repeat it together out loud. Reward them with time to play their favorite game.

CONCLUSION

During this class, students learned that God does not care about the size or appearance of people. Encourage them to feel safe and loved by the Lord and to trust in his loving protection. Pray with them before dismissing them and invite them to the next class.

NOTES:

LESSON 38

DAVID AND JONATHAN ARE GOOD FRIENDS

GENERAL ASPECTS

Biblical Basis: 1 Samuel 18:1-11; 19:1-10; 20:1-42

Memory Verse: *"The Lord does not look at the things people look at. People look at the outward appearance, but the Lord looks at the heart"* (1 Samuel 16:7).

Lesson Objective: To develop a desire to have friends that love and trust God.

TEACHER'S PREPARATION

In 1 Samuel 18:1-11, we read about the friendship of David and Jonathan, one of the most noble friendships in the Bible. In this first encounter, we see the link between these two true friends. Jonathan "loved David as himself," and made a promise to him, giving him his cape and armor. This attitude could symbolize Jonathan giving David his (Jonathan's) right to the throne.

In 1 Samuel 20:1-42, there are two very important themes: first, the friendship of these two young men, and second, David's fear of Saul's madness.

David and Jonathan understood the danger and adversity they faced, so they decided to promise each other loyalty and friendship before the Lord. The love they felt for one another was genuine, and even though they knew they may not see each other again, they trusted that God was in control of their circumstances.

In the middle of the conflict, David and Jonathan bravely found each other to say good bye, affirming the love and they promise they had.

David had been running from Saul's sword for many years. Meanwhile, Jonathan bravely lived each day with a father who did not trust him, and whose deepest wish was to kill his best friend. This must have been a painful conflict for him. Still, Jonathan loved and honored his father. He could have prioritized his own interests and sought David's death with his father, but he knew he was doing what was right. Jonathan made a righteous decision and gained the admiration of many generations.

David is often seen as the hero of this period. In Jonathan, we have an example worthy of recognition as the model of a loyal and godly man.

ADAPTATION

Children find different ways to be accepted by their peers. Many invest many hours of their day playing with their neighbors and friends from school. This is why the selection of friends can drastically influence their lives. Choosing friends that can help them grow in their walk with the Lord is very important during this critical stage of development.

This lesson will help students understand the importance of loving God and choosing friends who do the same.

LESSON DEVELOPMENT

Introduction

Ask some volunteers to tell the class about their best friends. They can also bring in pictures or invite them to class.

It is important that they say how they chose their best friend and what they enjoy doing together.

When they finish, congratulate them. Tell them that today's story is about two friends who loved each other very much.

DEVELOPMENT OF THE BIBLE STORY

Allow your students to sit how they please, and they can sit with their friends. Tell them that the story is about David and his friend Jonathan. They should pay attention because their friendship was so strong.

Tell the story with the Bible in your hand. Do not read the whole passage; only read the key verses.

Use what you have or can make to illustrate your story as you tell it. On a large piece of construction paper, write the word "friends," cut out the letters that spell it out, and tell the children to stick a letter onto the board every time you say the word "friends" in the story.

We also suggest that you show your students some fabric to represent a cape, as well as a toy sword.

Let them know what these symbols represent. An option for this moment is for students to make crowns and a sword and exchange them with a classmate as gifts.

APPLICATION TO DAILY LIFE

Through this story, students understand that friendship is a something that God has given us, and we should grow it. When we love our friends, we are obeying God's commands.

David loved Jonathan in spite of the fact that he was the son of the man who wanted to kill him. We should also love our friends, even if they make mistakes.

ACTIVITIES

Who is a Good Friend?

Give the worksheets to your students, along with colored pencils.

Tell your students to look at the drawing carefully, and to choose which of the children in the picture they would like to have as friends. Then, ask them to color the ones that they chose.

Then discuss as a class why they colored the ones that they did.

A Story of Friendship

Look at the drawings at the top of the second page of the worksheet with your students; have crayons or colored pencils ready. Ask them what they think is happening in the drawing. Facilitate a discussion about the situation using the following questions:

- ✘ In what different ways could this story end?
- ✘ What would have happened if Sebastian had agreed to go to the pond?
- ✘ What would have happened if Sebastian had not agreed to go to the pond?
- ✘ If Sebastian had agreed to do what Anthony wanted, would this have been right or wrong?
- ✘ Would a true friend do something dangerous just to please his friend? Why?

Allow your students to draw a happy ending to the story in the blank space that's provided.

Clarify that in the Bible story, Jonathan stood up against his father to defend David; he kept secrets with his friend and disobeyed his father's orders to kill him. Make sure your students understand that Jonathan and David were adults, not children. Children should obey their parents, since this is a commandment from God.

Nevertheless, take into account that not all of your students' parents are Christians. Be very careful in explaining to them that when their parents ask them to do something that is not right or pleasing to God, they should pray and seek counsel.

Emphasize that they should not keep their friends' secrets when it can be dangerous (saying bad words, smoking, stealing, etc..)

Let's Choose Our Friends

Provide pencils for your students and read the instructions on the worksheet for this activity.

Tell your students that choosing a friend is very important and can be a very difficult decision.

Ask, "Do you remember what the memory verse teaches us about this subject?" (We should not choose our friends based on physical appearance, but on their character.) "It takes some time to know what a person is like on the inside. Here are some ideas that will help you pick good friends." Give them time to fill in the blanks by using words from the word bank.

Friendship Cards

You will need blank sheets of paper, crayons, markers, stamps, stickers, scissors, and glue. Help your students make simple cards for their friends. They can decorate them however they please and write on them a memory verse or something special. When they finish, have them put the cards in envelopes and give them to whoever they have made them for. If you have time, allow them to make more than one card.

MEMORIZATION

This activity can be completed in groups or individually. You will need the verse written on construction paper, as well as scissors. Depending on whether the activity is individual or in groups, give the verse to the students so they can cut it out word by word (or prepare this beforehand). Allow them to place the words in the correct order as they memorize them.

CONCLUSION

Briefly review what the students have learned in their lessons on the life of David, and invite them to your next class to learn about how this young man showed mercy to someone who mistreated him.

Pray for your students' prayer requests and ask God to help your students be good friends.

LESSON 39

DAVID SHOWS MERCY

GENERAL ASPECTS

Biblical Basis: 1 Samuel 24 y 26

Memory Verse: *"The Lord does not look at the things people look at. People look at the outward appearance, but the Lord looks at the heart"* (1 Samuel 16:7).

Lesson Objective: To teach students that God's desire is that we show love and mercy to all people, even those who offend and hurt us.

TEACHER'S PREPARATION

When David and Saul were about to meet (23:26), the king was aggressive and David was a vulnerable fugitive. Now, David is safe in his hiding place and Saul is in danger and does not know it.

David had the opportunity, motivation and time to hurt Saul, but he did not do it, even though he knew that the king would kill him if he found him. When he showed him the piece of his cape, the king recognized that he had escaped death by David's mercy, who in his own words, was more just than himself.

In 1 Samuel 26, we see Saul again following David. This smart young man entered the king's campsite, stole his spear and canteen and left unscathed. The spear symbolized Saul's security and authority, and now this symbol of power was in the hands of his enemy.

God put Saul and all of his camp into a deep sleep. This supernatural action is a demonstration of God interceding for David and against Saul.

Chapter 24 and 26 reveal the purity of David's heart and the mercy he showed toward his enemy. In both chapters, we see God protecting David's life, and that vengeance belongs to the Lord. We should not hurt others, even when they are acting wrongly.

In our society, it is common for people to take justice into their own hands or seek revenge. Nevertheless, the children of God have a different perspective.

David had two opportunities to kill Saul. Who would blame him? It would have been in self-defense. But he showed mercy and chose not to hurt Saul because he was anointed by God.

ADAPTATION

Students have a strong sense of justice and are very sensitive to being treated unjustly. Many feel they should respond in the same way that they are hurt, and hold grudges or negative thoughts.

The mercy that David showed Saul shows another way of resolving conflict. Help them to understand that David's actions were a sign of strength and not weakness.

David showed mercy because he knew that God is the only judge. This trust can signify a new experience for them. Children wish to see immediate justice. Their concept of time is limited, and they want answers in the short-term. Knowing that God will judge all according to their acts will give them a new perspective.

LESSON DEVELOPMENT

Introduction

What Happens Next?

Give your students the 2nd page of the worksheet for this lesson, along with colored pencils. Ask them to look at the pictures and read the dialogue. Ask them what they think is happening in the story. In the blank square, have them draw the ending that they would like to see happen.

Talk to them about what it means to seek vengeance on someone who has hurt them. Tell them that in today's story, they will learn what David did when given the opportunity to take vengeance on the king who wanted him dead.

DEVELOPMENT OF THE BIBLE STORY

Review with your students what they have learned about David's life over the last several weeks.

Help them understand the context of the story. David was fleeing because king Saul wanted to kill him. He had spent a lot of time hiding in caves, far from his family. Nevertheless, he had no grudge in his heart against Saul.

Tell the Bible story and if possible, show pictures that will illustrate the story's events. If you wish, use the worksheet as a visual aid.

APPLICATION TO DAILY LIFE

In advance, cut out two red hearts for each student; glue or tape them together by the edges leaving them open enough on top to form a sort of envelope. Cut out various smaller hearts that will fit inside.

During the class, ask your students to help write on the board a list of qualities that David exhibited. Add to the list qualities that God likes to see in people's lives: kindness, honesty, trust, etc.

Distribute the small hearts to the children so they can write on them the qualities that they want God to see in them. They can choose from the qualities on David's list or from the additional list. Place the smaller hearts inside the heart envelope and make sure they have written their names on their envelopes. Encourage them to follow David's good example, and by doing so they will please God.

ACTIVITIES

David Shows Mercy

You will need worksheets for each student for this lesson, scissors, and glue.

Instruct your students to cut the strip of drawings from the CUTOUT section for this activity. Then, have them cut along the black parallel lines in the middle of the worksheet. Help them weave the strip of drawings from behind in between the black lines. Encourage them to move the strip and see the two ways in which David showed love and mercy towards Saul.

Review

Allow your students to review the story using the worksheet they have just completed. Tell them what happened and think of what could have happened if David had acted differently. Remind them that David chose not to hurt the king, but to show him mercy, even when Saul was trying to kill him.

Use these question to reinforce the lesson:

- ✘ Why was Saul chasing David?
- ✘ Where was Saul when David cut a piece of his robe?
- ✘ What did David take from Saul's campsite?
- ✘ Why was David merciful?
- ✘ Should we be merciful to people who hurt us?

MEMORIZATION

You will need construction paper, scissors, glue, or tape.

Prepare in advance a crown that will fit your students' heads, so they can wear it. Use the next activity to help them memorize 1 Samuel 16:7.

Have your students sit in a circle, then choose one to stand in the middle. Tell the one who is in the middle to close their eyes, wait a little and then say "Stop!" The students in the circle will pass the crown. When the student in the middle says "stop!", the student with the crown in his hands should put it on and recite the verse. Then that student will be in the middle and will say "stop." If you wish, you can allow the students to ask someone to help them remember the verse.

CONCLUSION

Invite your students to be merciful throughout the week with people who do not treat them fairly. Remind them that David's example teaches us to live according to God's will, being loving to those around us, including those who offend us.

As an introduction to the last lesson, "David Keeps His Promise," announce to your students that you will bring a surprise next week. It does not have to be expensive, it can be a sweet treat, a bookmark, or a pencil.

To finish, lead your group in prayer and pray for specific prayer requests. If possible, contact them throughout the week and talk to their parents about how their children are applying Biblical truths to their daily lives.

NOTES:

LESSON 40

DAVID KEEPS HIS PROMISES

GENERAL ASPECTS

Biblical Basis: 2 Samuel 9

Memory Verse: *"The Lord does not look at the things people look at. People look at the outward appearance, but the Lord looks at the heart"* (1 Samuel 16:7).

Lesson Objective: That students will learn that they should keep their promises to God, as David did.

TEACHER'S PREPARATION

In spite of the conflicts with King Saul and his descendants, David never forgot the promise of friendship that he shared with Jonathan. But Jonathan had already died.

David was searching for someone in the royal family to whom he could favor, and thus fulfill the promise he had made with his friend Jonathan. Ziba, a man who had been a servant in the house of Saul, told David that Jonathan still had a living son named Mephibosheth who had lame feet.

Mephibosheth was five years old when his father died (2 Samuel 4:4). When his nurse heard that Jonathan had died, she took the child and fled to keep him safe; but because she was in such a hurry, she dropped the child and he had lame feet from then on. When Mephibosheth learned that the king was looking for him, he feared for his life. In those times, new kings generally assured their ascendancy to the throne by killing all descendants of the previous king. It was not simple for David to take the throne of Israel, as he was constantly confronted by Ish-bosheth, one of Jonathan's younger brothers (2 Samuel 1-4).

Nevertheless, King David fulfilled the promise he had made to Jonathan and mercifully gave Mephibosheth all of the land that had belonged to his grandfather Saul.

David not only gave Mephibosheth all of his family's land, but invited him to be a part of his own family, asking him to eat at his table "like one of the king's sons."

ADAPTATION

In our society, promises are easily broken. Political leaders, television characters, and even members of our own families do not fulfill their promises. Maybe this is not a relevant theme for many people. Actually, many of our students, or we ourselves, have been confronted with a broken promise.

But promises were not meant to be broken, because to do so has consequences: we can lose the trust of others, as well as our integrity.

The children of God make promises as well. The difference is that when we fulfill them, we are obeying his laws. Fulfilling our word implies compassion and integrity. Help your students see David as an example of integrity in fulfilling his promise.

LESSON DEVELOPMENT

Introduction

Ask your students if they remember the promise you made them last week. Express how important it is for people to keep their promises.

Hand out the small gifts you have brought and ask how they would have felt if you had broken your promise.

Based on their responses, talk about the importance of doing what we promise. Today's story tells us of an important promise that David made to Jonathan, one he kept even when Jonathan was dead.

DEVELOPMENT OF THE BIBLE STORY

Remind your students of the lesson they learned about David and Jonathan's friendship. Emphasize the promise they made before they parted.

As you tell the story, allow your students to share their experiences concerning the topic and use them as examples.

As a visual aid, you can use figures to represent David and Mephibosheth, or make the booklet found on the student worksheet ahead of time to illustrate the story.

APPLICATION TO DAILY LIFE

Through today's story, students learned the importance of keeping their promises. Encourage them to imitate David's example and to be honest in doing that which they promise to.

Tell them, "When we promise something, we are giving our word, and people put their trust in us. What happens if we do not keep our promises?"

Listen to their response and finish by emphasizing that God loves it when His children keep their promises.

ACTIVITIES

The Promise of a Friend

You will need the worksheet from the student workbook, scissors, and a stapler or glue.

Help the students to cut out, fold, and put together the booklet, "The Promise of a Friend" as the instructions in the book indicate. Before stapling or gluing the book, make sure that the pages are in the correct order.

After you have finished, ask the following questions:

- ✘ What was your favorite part of today's story?
- ✘ What do you think God wants us to learn through this story? (Listen to their responses and lead the discussion.)

To conclude the activity, allow students to write their name on their booklets and take them home so they can tell others the story of David and Mephibosheth.

Keeping Your Promises

Have your students sit in a circle and tell them, "David kept the promise he made to his friend Jonathan, by taking care of his son, Mephibosheth. Now let's think about the promises we have made and should keep. I will begin by telling you a promise I have made and want to keep, then I will pass this ball to one of you. That person will share a promise that they want to keep. When you are done sharing, you may pass the ball to someone else who has not yet had a turn."

Use this game to allow your students to express themselves.

Review Game

Ask the following questions to review this unit's lessons about David. Divide your class into two groups. Each group should choose a captain who will share their answers on behalf of the group. Each correct answer will be worth five points. If a group does not know the answer, the other group will have a chance to answer the question to earn points.

1. What was David's job when he lived in Bethlehem?
2. What was the name of the servant of God who anointed David as king?
3. Who did David confront with his slingshot and five stones?
4. How did King Saul feel about David?
5. What was the name of David's best friend, and who was his dad?
6. Where did David and his men hide?
7. When King Saul entered the cave, what did David's men want to do to him?
8. What did David do instead of killing Saul?
9. What was the name of Jonathan's son, who David helped?
10. Repeat this unit's memory verse.

MEMORIZATION

Since this is the last class of the unit, prepare some prizes for those students who have learned the memory verse. You can give them crowns or paper hearts with the verse written on them. Allow time for all who wish to recite the verse to do so and to share with the class what they have learned.

CONCLUSION

With your class, briefly review the lessons from this unit and leave some time for them to share which stories impacted them the most.

Emphasize the importance of following David's example in their daily life. Like them, David was just a kid when God chose him to be the king of his people. Nevertheless, this simple shepherd became a powerful and respectable king.

They too can do great things in the hands of God.

Encourage them to place their trust in God and to obey His Word.

Before dismissing them, pray with them and repeat the memory verse together.

NOTES:

YEAR 1 UNIT IX

JESUS TEACHES US HOW TO LIVE

Biblical Basis: Luke 2:41-52; 9:51-56; Mark 4:35-41; 12:38-44

Unit Theme Verse: "... *Love the Lord your God with all your heart and with all your soul and with all your mind*" (Matthew 22:37).

PURPOSE OF THIS UNIT

This unit will help your students:

- ✘ Discover what Jesus taught through his words and example.
- ✘ Learn to love and trust God by obeying their parents.
- ✘ Please God by following Jesus' example and obeying his commands.
- ✘ Realize that it is much easier to love and obey God by following Jesus' example.
- ✘ Learn to trust God when they are fearful.
- ✘ Learn to forgive people who have hurt them.
- ✘ Give God the best gifts they can give Him: their love and service.

UNIT LESSONS

Lesson 41: Jesus Obeys His Parents

Lesson 42: Jesus Calms the Storm

Lesson 43: God Forgives

Lesson 44: Jesus Honors a Widow

WHY WE NEED TO TEACH THIS UNIT

This unit will help students see the connection between "attitudes" and "actions." They will discover that Jesus showed that some attitudes and actions, such as trust, obedience to parents, forgiveness, and sincere love are pleasing to God.

Students will also learn about the importance of being obedient to their parents. God considered it so important that He included it in the Ten Commandments. Jesus, the very Son of God, was obedient to His earthly parents, Joseph and Mary.

In lesson 42 (Jesus Calms the Storm), students will see how Jesus is in control of every situation. Because they are young, they are sometimes fearful of their circumstances. This lesson will teach them not to be afraid and to trust in God.

Additionally, students' social relations will expand as they themselves grow. They have left the security of their homes and attend school for many hours a day; their world has been opened to new ways of relating to others.

Learning to have good relationships with others is not always easy for students. For this reason, it is important to teach them how to be kind to others (friends, family, neighbors, etc.).

Through studying these lessons, your students will begin searching for ways to be like Jesus.

LESSON 41

JESUS OBEYS HIS PARENTS

GENERAL ASPECTS

Biblical Basis: Luke 2:41-52

Memory Verse: *"Love the Lord your God with all your heart and with all your soul and with all your mind"* (Matthew 22:37).

Lesson Objective: To help students know that God wants them to obey Him.

TEACHER'S PREPARATION

In Luke 2:41-52, we are told about one of the unique events of Jesus' childhood that appear in the Bible, besides His birth and the visit of the three wise men. There are many legends about his childhood that are not based on scripture. What distinguishes these legends from the Gospels is their emphasis on the uniqueness of Jesus as a child. Many depict him as exhibiting extraordinary powers.

This story contrasts greatly with these legends. When Jesus was 12 years old, He was developing in all areas of his life, including His knowledge concerning His mission on earth and His relationship to God the Father. People were amazed at His vast knowledge (Luke 2:47). However, this passage clearly shows that the teachers of the law were not aware that the young boy who was asking so many questions was fully God and fully man.

When Joseph and Mary found Jesus, their reaction was one of relief. Jesus seemed surprised that His parents didn't know where He was. Still, we read that He submitted to the authority of His parents. He obeyed them, giving us an example of the way we should submit to our earthly parents.

ADAPTATION

In this day and age, obedience seems to be out of style. Some books, television shows, and magazines portray parents as negative figures. Respect for them and their authority seems to be under pressure.

Students need to know the importance of obeying their parents. God considered this so important that He included it as one of the Ten Commandments. The writers of the New Testament also reaffirm the importance of this obedience. Your students can learn that Jesus, the very Son of God, obeyed Joseph and Mary. As history shows, it was not always easy, but he was always obedient.

LESSON DEVELOPMENT

Introduction

A Job To Do

Play this game so that students can reflect on the chores or duties that they do in their homes. They must follow the instructions. After giving most of the instructions, ask for some volunteers to supplement the activity by giving additional commands:

- ✘ Stand up if you make your bed in the morning.
- ✘ Clap if you wash the dishes.
- ✘ Jump three times if you take care of a family pet.
- ✘ Wave your hands if you pick up your toys.
- ✘ Touch your toes if you take out the trash.
- ✘ Hop twice on one foot if you clean your room.
- ✘ Say "Yes" if you help set the table before meals.
- ✘ Pat yourself on the back if you care for a younger brother or sister.

After the game, ask your students, "How do you feel when your parents ask you to do any of these chores?" Encourage students to be honest with their responses.

Say, "Sometimes it is easy to obey our parents, but other times it is not that simple. Let's see what Jesus teaches us about obedience."

DEVELOPMENT OF THE BIBLE STORY

Using visual aids during lesson development is very stimulating for children because they can both see and hear the story.

If you do not have access to visual aids in your classroom, consider in advance alternate ways to elaborate on the lesson. You could use magazine or newspaper clippings that display places where there are a lot of people, parades, celebrations, etc. This will give your students an example of the situation that Joseph and Mary were in when they lost sight of Jesus.

Tell the story in a way that will help your students imagine the experience that Jesus and His family had.

APPLICATION TO DAILY LIFE

We have used this story to show students that Jesus, even as the Son of God, was always obedient to His parents during His time on earth. The need to obey is very important for your students to understand.

Highlight the fact that obedience, although we don't always like it, is a vital part of discipline and well-balanced personal growth.

Obedience Reminders

Distribute worksheets, colored pencils or crayons, scissors, glue, and envelopes to your students. If you do not have envelopes, you can make them using white paper and glue. (If you are making copies, be sure to copy both pages of the worksheet and glue them together or copy both sides so that the scripture verses are on the back of the Obedience Reminders. Or have your students write the verses on the back of the Obedience Reminders.)

Read the instructions aloud and help your students cut out their "Obedience Reminders." Ask them to place their reminders in their envelope and take them home to talk about them with their parents so that they can decide together how the child can be obedient. Later, have them write down what they decided to do. This will serve as a constant reminder to be obedient.

ACTIVITIES

Jesus Obey His Parents

For this activity, you will need a blackboard and chalk or paper and markers.

Before class, draw a rectangle and divide it into seven equal parts. Mark the first rectangle as Jerusalem, and the last one as Nazareth. Say, "Let's see if we can take Jesus from Jerusalem to Nazareth by answering questions about the story." Ask the following questions and each time one is answered correctly, color in one section of the rectangle. If they cannot answer a question, answer it for them and move on to the next question. Continue playing until all the sections have been colored in. If necessary, repeat some of the questions:

- ✘ Where did Joseph, Mary, and their family celebrate the Passover? (In Jerusalem.)
- ✘ What happened to Jesus on this trip? (He was left behind.)
- ✘ What did Joseph and Mary do when they noticed that Jesus was not with them? (They returned to Jerusalem to find him.)
- ✘ How do you think they felt when they couldn't find Jesus? (Fearful, disappointed, worried.)
- ✘ Where did they find Jesus? (In the temple.)
- ✘ What was Jesus doing in the temple? (Talking with the teachers of the law, asking and answering questions.)
- ✘ What was surprising about the answers that Jesus gave? (They were very wise.)
- ✘ What did Mary say to Jesus? (We have been looking for you everywhere.)
- ✘ How did Jesus respond to his mother? (Didn't you know that I would be in my father's house?)
- ✘ What did Mary and Joseph ask Jesus to do? (To return home with them.)
- ✘ What did Jesus do? (He obeyed.)

MEMORIZATION

Write on the chalkboard some of the letters of the words from the memory verse that students will learn for this Unit. Write the remaining letters on small pieces of paper and place them in a bag. Ask some volunteers to take a letter out of the bag and see if they can correctly place the letter in the words.

They must place the letter in the correct place within the verse. When they have finished, read the verse together and repeat it several times.

When Obeying is Dangerous

Some parents use Biblical teachings about obedience to exploit or abuse their children. While you work with your students, be sensitive and patient with those children who respond with anger or anxiety. If any of your students suggest that they are being abused, report your suspicion to a pastor or youth minister.

Ephesians 6:1-4 lists the responsibilities that children have towards their parents, and those that parents have towards their children when it says, "[1]Children, obey your parents in the Lord, for this is right. [2] 'Honor your father and mother'—which is the first commandment with a promise— [3] 'so that it may go well with you and that you may enjoy long life on the earth.' [4]Fathers, do not exasperate your children; instead, bring them up in the training and instruction of the Lord."

It is sad that child abuse occurs at all, regardless of race or social status. Pray for your students and for their families.

CONCLUSION

Make sure that all your students finish their work and take their belongings home. Encourage them to obey their parents throughout the week and to review their memory verse. Before dismissing your students, form a circle and pray for each of your students by name.

LESSON 42
JESUS CALMS THE STORM

GENERAL ASPECTS

Biblical Basis: Mark 4:35-41

Memory Verse: *"Love the Lord your God with all your heart and with all your soul and with all your mind"* (Matthew 22:37).

Lesson Objective: That students will learn to trust God when they feel afraid.

TEACHER'S PREPARATION

This Bible story is set in the sea of Galilee, a lake of fresh water measuring 26 kilometers long and 14 kilometers wide. It is located in the Jordan Valley at 200 meters below sea level. It is surrounded by hills. When the wind blows, the hills create a funnel that reaches the water and the wind breaks out in full force. The sea of Galilee is famous for its violent and unforeseen storms; even experienced fishermen can be surprised by them.

The majority of Jesus' ministry on earth happened near this lake. Some of his disciples, such as Simon Peter, were experienced fishermen and understood the danger of being in the lake during an intense storm. This knowledge increased their fear, and they couldn't understand how Jesus could be sleeping during the storm.

Mark 4:35-41 asks us two questions:

- Who is Jesus?
- Do you trust Him?

The firmness and brevity of Jesus' command to the wind and the sea shows the sureness that He had everything under His control. Jesus' control over the forces of nature display His divine authority. The words "Peace! Be still!" give us great hope. In the worst of problems, from worrying about our day, to facing death, these same words can comfort all those who listen to the voice of the Son of God.

ADAPTATION

During this stage of life, children have many fears. This lesson will help them to work constructively with those fears and learn to trust in God. It is important to recognize that fear is not inherently bad. It is a good emotion given by God that can protect us from many types of danger. But when fear paralyzes us or threatens our trust in God, it can become very dangerous.

The miracle of calming the storm shows us the authority of Jesus over all creation. This authority should inspire our confidence in him. This does not mean that children who trust in God are invincible and are protected from all danger, but that it is God who has authority over everything that exists, and He is with them regardless of what they face.

LESSON DEVELOPMENT

Introduction

For the introduction, you will need sheets of paper and colored pencils or crayons.

Ask your students if they ever experience fear. Allow some time for them to respond, and then give them the sheets of paper to draw on. Ask them to draw a situation that has made them afraid in the past. Ask some volunteers to share their drawings with the rest of their classmates and explain what they drew.

Say, "Today we will learn about a time when Jesus' disciples felt afraid. Let's see what He told them about fear."

DEVELOPMENT OF THE BIBLE STORY

Provide used or recycled sheets of paper to the students, paper cones, newspaper, paper bags, or cellophane that will not be used for other purposes. Tell the students they can use these materials to make noises that sound like the storm from the Bible story. Crumpling up paper and bags can make sounds similar to thunder, and blowing through paper cones can mimic the sound of the wind.

As you tell the story, let the students make these sounds when the part with the storm comes, and ask them how they would feel in a similar situation.

Encourage them to enjoy the silence and calm that the disciples felt when Jesus commanded the storm to stop. Invite your students to participate as actors. These activities are enjoyable for the children and can reinforce the lesson.

Prepare a row of chairs and tape some newspaper

around it to simulate the walls of the boat. Some children can play the disciples and can use brooms as oars, while one can play Jesus, sleeping under a blanket. The rest of the students can continue making the sounds of the wind and thunder. Meanwhile, narrate the story as your students act it out.

APPLICATION TO DAILY LIFE

Compare the fear of the disciples with the fear that your students feel in the face of difficult situations; for example, being in a dark room, going to a new school, sleeping alone in a room, etc.

It is good to remind them that God is the creator of all and He exercises complete control over His creation, including that which gives your students fear.

ACTIVITIES

The Storm is Calmed

Give your students the worksheet, scissors, and glue. Cut out the strip that says "Trust" from the CUTOUT section at the back of the student book.

Read together the paragraph found on the worksheet and fold the page on the dotted line. Afterwards, help your students to carefully cut along the black lines to make ten openings, then unfold the page and weave the "trust" strip through the openings, starting from the right side. Show them how to move the strip from side to side to simulate ocean waves.

Trust Reminder: Hidden Message

Have you Bible open to Psalm 56:3 and ask your students to find this verse.

Turn the worksheet over and tell them "We should all exercise our trust in God daily so that it can grow. King David, whom we studied in the last unit, was a man who put his trust in God, and he spoke of this trust when he wrote this beautiful psalm that we will now read."

Let a volunteer read the verse and then ask the following questions:

- ✘ Did David say, "I'm never afraid"? (No, he said, "When I am afraid".)
- ✘ What can we learn from what David said about fear? (We all feel fear and that's natural. However, it is wrong to let ourselves be overcome by fear.)
- ✘ What did David do when he was afraid? (He trusted in God.)
- ✘ What do you think God wants us to do when we are afraid? (Put our trust in Him.)

Give your students time to choose their favorite color and to color the spaces that have a dot. This way they will discover the hidden message.

Boats of Trust

For this activity you can use any kind of recycled material (newspaper, colored sheets, felt cutouts, clean milk cartons) glue, scissors, tape, crayons and colored pencils.

Give your students the materials and encourage them to use their imagination to create a little boat like the one Jesus was in during the storm. If they need help, work with them.

When they have finished, they can display their boats and invite members of the congregation to view them.

MEMORIZATION

To review the memory verse, have your students sit facing forward and ask them to keep their eyes closed. Write the memory verse on the board. When you finish, ask your students to open their eyes and read it. Have them close their eyes and when they do, erase some of the key words. Ask them what happened and see if they can repeat the complete verse. Continue in this manner until the verse is completely erased.

Give your students the opportunity to repeat the verse individually and in small groups.

CONCLUSION

Before dismissing the class, make sure that you give your students all the work they've done in class and invite them to attend the next class. Mention the topic for next week's lesson and pray for the needs of your students.

NOTES:

LESSON 43

GOD FORGIVES

GENERAL ASPECTS

Biblical Basis: Luke 9:51-56

Memory Verse: *"Love the Lord your God with all your heart and with all your soul and with all your mind"* (Matthew 22:37).

Lesson Objective: To help students to forgive people who have sinned against them.

TEACHER'S PREPARATION

Jesus was about to finish His mission on earth and was on His way to Jerusalem, where He would suffer the punishment for the sins of the world. During the journey, he sent his disciples to prepare to stop and rest in a Samaritan village.

When the Samaritans found out that Jesus and His disciples were headed to Jerusalem, the political and religious center of the Jewish people, they denied them a place to stay for the night. This was a serious insult. Hospitality towards travelers was integral to these ancient cultures. Enmity among Jews and Samaritans had a long history due to constant racial and cultural conflicts.

The disciples were angry at being treated this way by the Samaritans, and encouraged Jesus to punish them. But he showed them again that he was the Son of God. They had always heard that the Messiah would end the enmity between the Jews and the Samaritans. However, they believed that this would be by punishment and severe orders.

When the Samaritans rejected Jesus and his apostles, it seemed logical to them that He would punish them. Instead, Jesus had other plans and rebuked them. They knew He was the Christ, but they had not understood that His mission was to forgive and redeem, not to destroy, and that He had come to the world to give grace and forgiveness, not punishment and judgment.

ADAPTATION

Social skills of children grow as they age. They have left the security of their home to attend school during a large part of their day. Their world has opened and taught them new ways of relating to others. Learning to relate well to others is not always easy for them. As they make friends, it is likely that they will experience conflict. Kindness is a healthy way to deal with conflict. Being kind to others (friends, family, and sometimes enemies) is essential to constructing and maintaining social relationships.

For small children, it can be hard to be kind to those who have mistreated them. Generally, they react aggressively and do not think before they act. They follow their impulses and are guided by their emotions. Other times they do not know how to respond and they feel inferior and vulnerable.

This lesson is very similar to the one about David, who decided to treat King Saul with kindness, even though he was his enemy. Studying this topic again will help to reinforce what they learned, and to understand this Biblical principle from the perspective of the New Testament.

LESSON DEVELOPMENT

Introduction

You Decide!

This game will help you prepare students to listen to this Bible story and apply it to their daily lives. Students will take turns acting as the principal of a school. You will represent a teacher who is asking him or her what to do with the following students:

1. A fifth grader stole a younger student's lunch money.
2. A fourth grader ran through the halls and knocked over a student who was on crutches.
3. A first grader hid one of her classmate's pencils.
4. A second grader shared all of his friend's secrets with the class.
5. A third grader made fun of someone's clothes.

Be careful not to mention names; just say "a boy or a girl." The student representing the principal should decide the punishment that the guilty child deserves. After all the punishments have been decided, ask the students how they would feel if they were one of the guilty students and had to complete the punishment assigned by the principal.

Tell them that when one person hurts another person, many people will want them to be punished. Sometimes, the person who was hurt decides to take revenge on the person who hurt them. This is referred to as "an eye for an eye and a tooth for a tooth." Ask, "Can anyone give me an example of this?" Allow the group to respond. Mention that in the Bible story, some people treated Jesus badly, and today we will learn how He responded.

DEVELOPMENT OF THE BIBLE STORY

Help your students understand the context in which today's Bible story takes place. Jesus and His disciples were completing a long trip. They had walked many miles on rocky trails and they were tired and hungry. During their journey, the Teacher, Jesus, had healed the sick, cast out demons, and helped many people. It is only logical that he felt tired and wanted to rest.

In addition to all of that, Jesus knew that these would be his last few days on earth before suffering the punishment for all the sins of the world on the cross, and his heart was troubled.

Tell the story to your students and invite them to read it in their own Bible.

APPLICATION TO DAILY LIFE

This story is a clear example of the humility and simplicity of Jesus. Forgiveness is difficult, whether we are children or adults; however, this attitude is even more difficult in the lives of children when we try to teach them to forgive but they do not perceive a forgiving spirit in our attitude. In addition, society has ingrained, especially in boys, that forgiveness, rather than revenge, is a sign of weakness.

Students should know what Jesus taught about forgiveness so that they can apply it to their lives. Knowing that Jesus, the very Son of God, forgave his transgressors will help the students develop a spirit of forgiveness from an early age.

ACTIVITIES

Who Says What?

Give your students the worksheets for this lesson, crayons, and pencils. Review the Bible story by reading the phrases in the bubbles and decide which character said them. Let the children read the phrases from left to right and draw a line from the bubbles to the characters that said the phrases.

What Are You Thinking?

Looking at the illustrations on the student worksheets, start a discussion about what is happening in each picture. Have your students create a story based on the illustration and talk about how the mistreated children should act. Ask and encourage questions, and invite your students to answer them according to the Bible passage.

As they express their viewpoints, encourage them to remember that Jesus teaches us to forgive, even when others are not kind to us.

Scrambled Letters

Prepare in advance on sheets of paper or pieces of cardboard the letters that form the word "forgiveness," and have tape ready. Each letter should be repeated according to the number of teams you will have in class. Divide the students into teams of 11 and give them a set of 11 letters scrambled up. (If your class is smaller, students can have more than one letter.) With the tape, they should attach the letters to their chest.

When they are ready, they will form a circle as a song plays. When the music ends, teams should form the word "forgiveness." The first team to complete the challenge wins and they get to write the word on the board or tape the letters to the wall.

MEMORIZATION

For this activity, you will need to write the memory verse on a piece of paper or cardboard and then cut it into strips. Then put the strips in a box or bag.

Mix them up and allow your students to take them out one by one and put them in order. If they succeed, congratulate them and award them with a treat if you can.

CONCLUSION

As a review, write on the board in large letters, "What is Forgiveness?" and surround it with drawings of clouds, circles, balloons (whatever is easy to draw), and inside the circles write the following words: fight, revenge, love others, forget, continue being a friend, help, hit, be kind.

Instruct your students to erase the words that don't show an attitude of forgiveness. When they are done, only words that put into practice what Jesus taught about forgiveness will remain.

Invite a volunteer to end the class in prayer.

LESSON 44

JESUS HONORS A WIDOW

GENERAL ASPECTS

Biblical Basis: Mark 12:38-44

Memory Verse: *"Love the Lord your God with all your heart and with all your soul and with all your mind"* (Matthew 22:37).

Lesson Objective: To teach students that love and service are the best gifts they can give to God.

TEACHER'S PREPARATION

During His ministry, Jesus emphasized on many occasions the grandeur of humble people and outcasts. Throughout the New Testament we find many passages that remind us that He honored humble people and used them for His service. For example, when He chose the lunch of a young boy to feed five thousand people, He used a young boy as the example to show His disciples who was the greatest, and also at the moment in which He compares the generosity of a poor widow with the arrogance and conceit of the Pharisees.

The very life of Jesus is an example of humility. He came to this world humbly, never expecting to be honored, and on the contrary, demonstrated a constant spirit of humility.

One day, Jesus was sitting in front of the ark of the offering and watched the townspeople place their money in it, as the rich men and the Pharisees boasted about how much they offered to God. He knew that there was no sincerity in the hearts of these men, and the only thing they wanted was to draw attention to themselves from those around them.

A very poor widow approached the ark of the offering and deposited two small coins of little value. Nevertheless, Jesus compared her offering with that of the religious leaders. They had offered large quantities of money, and had calculated their offerings according to the laws for offerings and tithes. Nevertheless, this woman gave everything she had, and all she had left.

Jesus knew the sincerity of this woman's offering and her confidence in God's provision for her needs. This served as a lesson for His disciples, and affirmed once more that the kingdom of heaven is not won by works, but by faith and love.

ADAPTATION

Children of this age do not have difficulty in accepting the love and mercy of God in their life. Indeed, they have doubts and questions, but their faith is sincere and selfless. They are aware of his love and divine care.

And they like to please God; for example by singing, praying, and worshiping together in the church. But sometimes, they feel limited by their age in what they can do. They don't have much money to offer, can't contribute much to church projects, or work as ministers or missionaries.

This lesson will help your students understand that God cares more about sincere and selfless love than material offerings. It is likely that the children will identify with the poor widow that did not have many resources to offer to God. Nevertheless, Jesus viewed this action as a sincere and loving gift. Through this lesson, they will learn different ways to show their love to God.

LESSON DEVELOPMENT

Introduction

Give each student a sheet of paper and colored pencils, and ask them to draw the best gift they can give to God. When they are finished, hang up the drawings and allow the students to come up and explain their pictures to their classmates. When all the drawings have been explained, tell them that today's lesson will be about a person who truly loved God and gave Him a beautiful gift.

DEVELOPMENT OF THE BIBLE STORY

Show your students two coins of little value in your right hand, and in the left hand, a large quantity bill. Ask them, "Which of these two offerings is more pleasing to God?" (Give them time to respond and clarify the questions or doubts that emerge as you relate the Bible story.)

Ask your students to think of the historical context in which the story is set. Explain that Jews would gather in synagogues (churches) to worship God the same way we do in church today. Inside the synagogue was a chest where money was collected; people would deposit their tithes and offerings there.

In that time, some very studious men, called Pharisees or teachers of the law, did not act according to the will of God. They also went to the synagogue and deposited their offerings, but they did not do this sincerely.

It is important that you make clear to your students that the quantity or value of our offering does not concern God, only the sincerity and love with which we give it. The Pharisees gave valuable offerings, not out of love for God, but so that people would admire them. In contrast, the poor widow wanted to show God her love and faith so she gave all she had, two small coins.

APPLICATION TO DAILY LIFE

Relate the Biblical truth to the daily life of your students. Let them give examples of ways in which they can give gifts to God (praying, worshiping, reading His word to others, obeying His commandments, etc.). Encourage them to always be sincere and to offer God the best of themselves with all their hearts.

ACTIVITIES

She Gave Everything She Had!

Give each of your students the worksheet that goes with this lesson, scissors, and an envelope or plastic bag. (If you make copies, be sure to copy the front and back of the worksheet on the same paper or glue the sheets together. Or you can write the verse on the back of the illustration.)

Ask your students what the illustration is referring to. After reviewing the Bible story, help them cut along the black lines to make a puzzle.

As the students work on the activity, emphasize the Biblical truth of this lesson by asking the following questions:

1. How much did the teachers of the law give? (A lot of money because they were wealthy.) Explain that they wanted to be noticed as they gave their offerings so they put lots of coins in the offering box so that it would make a lot of noise. They wanted people to say, "Look at all that they gave; they must really love God."
2. How much did the widow offer? (Two small coins, everything she had.)
3. Why do you think the widow gave everything she had? (Because she really loved God.)
4. How could she live if she had no money? (She trusted that God would provide for her.)

Ask the students to place their puzzle pieces on the table and to solve the puzzle to discover the text on the back of the drawing (Mark 12:43).

After reading the verse, put the puzzle pieces into the envelopes so that they can take them home and share the story with their family.

What Can I Give?

Prepare red pieces of construction paper or some similar paper with a heart drawn on it. Distribute them along with scissors, crayons or markers, and tape to your students.

Ask them to cut out the heart and to write on them some of the following phrases:

- ✘ When you pray, tell God how much you love Him.
- ✘ Write a letter to someone who is sick.
- ✘ Help your parents by doing chores at home.
- ✘ Obey God.
- ✘ Be kind to people that are mean to you.
- ✘ Help your teacher.
- ✘ Read the Bible.

When everyone is finished, help them stick their hearts in some visible part of the room, as a reminder of the gifts they can offer to God.

MEMORIZATION

Today is the last lesson in the unit, and surely most of the students will have learned the memory verse.

If possible, ask your pastor if the students can recite the verse and share the basic lessons they've learned from this unit with the congregation during the service.

CONCLUSION

Briefly review what has been taught over the course of the unit. Allow time for your students to remember the Bible stories and lessons. Invite them to the next class, and introduce the next unit.

Pray for the needs of your students. Contact their families to see how they are applying at home what they have learned in class.

YEAR 1 UNIT X

A FAITHFUL GOD AND A FAITHFUL SERVANT

Biblical Basis: 1 Kings 17:1-16; 18; 19; 2 Kings 2:1-18

Unit Theme Verse: "*...The prayer of a righteous person is powerful and effective*" (James 5:16b).

PURPOSE OF THIS UNIT

This unit will help your students:

- ✘ Discover that in every situation, God is faithful.
- ✘ Recognize that faithful people help in the work of God.
- ✘ Grow in their trust in God.
- ✘ Want to be faithful servants of God.
- ✘ Discover how God provides for our needs.
- ✘ Rely on God in times of need.

UNIT LESSONS

Lesson 45: God Provides for Elijah

Lesson 46: Who is God?

Lesson 47: God Strengthens Elijah

Lesson 48: God Continues His Work

WHY WE NEED TO TEACH THIS UNIT

At this age, children look for heroes to imitate and to admire. The Bible is full of valuable heroes; Elijah is one of them. God demonstrated through the life of Elijah that He is in control of everything that exists.

Elijah was a hero, but he was also a human being like us. Many times he felt exhausted; he had become a fearful man, discouraged and full of dismay. At other times he felt alone; he even said to God, "Enough is enough, Lord" (1 Kings 19:4). James 5:17 says that he was a man like us. This balance between heroism and humanity can make Elijah someone real for children to learn from.

The true hero in the story of Elijah is God. Help the children recognize that he is always acting, no matter how bad the situation. Your students will sometimes feel discouraged, so they need to learn to rely on a God who is in control.

God showed His power over evil on Mount Carmel. When Elijah was tired of fleeing from Jezebel, the Lord gave him rest, sustenance, and encouragement. He also showed Elijah that He is in control, even when circumstances change.

Help your students grow in the confidence that in every situation, God can do His will. He is the author of life; he made the world and everything in it.

LESSON 45

GOD PROVIDES FOR ELIJAH

GENERAL ASPECTS

Biblical Basis: 1 Kings 17:1-16

Memory Verse: "*The prayer of a righteous person is powerful and effective*" (James 5:16b).

Lesson Objective: To help students discover the different ways God provides for their needs.

TEACHER'S PREPARATION

There are three situations talked about in Chapter 17 of 1 Kings which show the triumph of God's power. The problem they all have in common is the possibility of death. The solution, which was given through miracles, is life. This lesson focuses on the first two situations. God provided for the needs of Elijah in different ways. He combined ordinary things with extraordinary ones to keep Elijah alive. For Elijah, these events within his ministry served as a time of preparation.

Elijah's disposition changes from being passive to active. In the first story, he simply obeys and God feeds him. In the second, he tells what God is going to do, remains under his protection and witnesses his great power.

Why would God send the crows to feed Elijah? These animals are distinguished by their lack of cleanliness, perhaps the food would have been unhealthy for him.

It is also very likely that the crows would not have been so willing to give the food to Elijah; they'd want to eat it themselves. But God was in control of the situation and ordered the crows to bring bread and meat to his servant.

In contrast to the bread and meat that the crows brought him, God used a very natural resource to give him water. He told him to drink from a stream. After he had drunk from the stream for awhile, because there was a tremendous drought, the stream dried up. But the one who caused the drought arranged everything for Elijah to have a roof over his head and food on his table.

Then God sent Elijah to Zarephath of Sidon, to the house of a widow. Here, God again provided for Elijah to have food to eat, unbelievably multiplying the widow's food while she cared for Elijah. Oil and flour are ordinary items, but the fact that they never ran out is extraordinary.

ADAPTATION

Many children are not aware of how their daily needs are being met. They see the food on the table and have a house to live in and think it is very natural. Sometimes they are more concerned about the style of a clothes they wear than about the warmth and protection that a home gives them; they do not take into account the provisions of God.

Help your students recognize that God is the giver of life by having created the world and all that dwells in it. Many people see how the Lord provides for them so they do not need extraordinary circumstances or miracles to eat or have shelter.

Use this lesson to help your students understand that it is God who supplies everything they need, depending on how he chooses to do it: in ordinary or extraordinary ways.

LESSON DEVELOPMENT

Introduction

What Do We Need?

Give your students the worksheet and tell them, "These drawings show us all kinds of things that people need and want. Circle what we need to survive and be healthy. Then, mark with an X the things we enjoy but we can live without." Allow the children time to think about this activity. Remind them to circle only what is necessary, not what makes life easier.

Ask, "How do we get everything we need?" (Listen to their answers. They will try to explain how their family gets them.) Guide the discussion and ask the children where they get their food, where they get their water, etc. Help them to discover that God gives us all that we need because He created the earth and all that is in it.

Tell them, "Now we understand that God gives us water, air, sun, food and plants, as well as the animals from which we get food, because he created everything. But sometimes we forget about his love and the way he cares for us. In today's Bible story, we will meet a person whom the Lord provided for in an extraordinary way, but at the same time, in a simple way. Let's see if you can figure out the difference between the two."

DEVELOPMENT OF THE BIBLE STORY

Consider inviting a member of your congregation to represent Elijah and tell the Bible story. Give them the Bible scripture passage (1 Kings 17:1-16) so that they can prepare properly.

If you prefer, narrate and illustrate the story using some pictures or drawings that you draw yourself based on the development of the story.

APPLICATION TO DAILY LIFE

To apply this lesson to daily life, bring to class some magazines featuring pictures of families, children and family activities. Give the magazines to the students and have them look for things that God provides to us so that we can live, such as food, water, family, parents, etc. As the children find the pictures, ask them to pass them on to others. Thank God for providing us with all that is good for us.

ACTIVITIES

How Did God Care For Elijah?

Have your students turn to the second page of their worksheets. They will need to cut out the shapes from the CUTOUT Section at the back of the student book and glue them in correct places on the worksheet. Then review the lesson with these questions:

- ✗ Where does Elijah appear in the drawing? (Near the stream of Querit.)
- ✗ How did God help Elijah? (God gave Elijah water from the stream.)
- ✗ What unusual way did God use to care for Elijah? (God had crows bring food to Elijah.)

Have your students follow the instructions on the worksheet.

Conclude this part of the lesson by saying, "God cared for Elijah in two different ways: one ordinary and one extraordinary. He also cares for us because he loves us and wants us to be happy."

Project: "Let's Do Something Extraordinary!"

Remind your students of the special ways God cared for Elijah. Tell them that they too can help others, and have them think about how they can could take food to people who need it.

Have your students collect bags, cans or boxes of food. They can ask their parents for imperishable foods to give to a family that needs them. (It would be a good idea to send a note home to their parents to tell them about your project.) Talk with your pastor about this project, and ask him about needs within your church and community.

Give several weeks for your students to collect these items. Set a designated place to put all the food together as it is brought in, and set a special date to deliver everything the children have collected.

Look for ways in which your students can help you distribute the food. Emphasize that they can help in a very simple and ordinary way to meet the needs of someone in need. The people who receive this help will feel that it was something extraordinary.

MEMORIZATION

On a white poster board, or a piece of good-sized paper, write in large letters the memory verse along with the Bible reference. Give your students the opportunity to decorate the poster. Provide colored pencils, markers and whatever you need to color and decorate it to your liking. When they have finished put it in a visible place in you classroom so that everyone can read the verse whenever they want to.

CONCLUSION

This is the first of four lessons that talks about the prophet Elijah. Invite your students to become familiar with this Bible hero by reading about his life during the week.

Encourage them to acknowledge God's provision for them and their families every day and thank Him for it.

Lead them in prayer thanking God for caring for them and for meeting their needs. Pray for specific requests within the group.

NOTES:

LESSON 46

WHO IS GOD?

GENERAL ASPECTS

Biblical Basis: 1 Kings 18

Memory Verse: "*The prayer of a righteous person is powerful and effective*" (James 5:16b).

Lesson Objective: To help students understand that God is unique and powerful.

TEACHER'S PREPARATION

Within the history of the people of Israel, we find that many times they were inclined to serve other gods. The appeal of worshiping false idols seemed irresistible. People were seduced by the worship of the Canaanite god of fertility. However, their loyalty was divided. They claimed to believe in God, but worshiped Baal.

Elijah called the people to be loyal only to God. He asked them, "How long will you waver between two opinions? If the Lord is God, follow him; but if Baal is God, follow him" (v.21).

This prophet knew very well the answer to his challenge; he had experienced innumerable times the mighty hand of God in his life, and suffered because of the disobedience and idolatry of the people.

What happened on Mount Carmel is an extraordinary example of the faith and trust that Elijah had in God. He was the only prophet of the Lord who was still alive, and it was his goal to show the king and the people the omnipotence of God.

The worship of Baal was backed by the highest levels of government, including the queen. His priests and prophets were counted by the hundreds. However, this was not important to Elijah; He served the living God, knew him personally and knew that it was He who controlled the situation.

Elijah's faith makes us think he was a hero, and to some extent he is. However, James 5:17 reminds us, "Elijah was a human being, even as we are." This implies that we too can have the faith like Elijah and prove with courage that God whom we serve is the one and only true God.

ADAPTATION

Your students are interested in learning more about God. At this age, many children easily accept what others tell them about the Lord. They are getting to experience different environments in which they are faced with people with new ideas and ways of thinking. At their school they will come to know different religions, even some that worship other gods.

It is very important that, within all this confusion of new religious beliefs that they face, they can be sure that God is the only Lord. They need to see the Lord in action and listen to stories where he shows himself to be Almighty. The confrontation of Elijah with the priests of Baal will help them understand the power and absolute sovereignty of God.

LESSON DEVELOPMENT

Introduction

Stick a large piece of cardboard or white paper on a wall in your classroom or on the wall, like a mural. In the middle of this write the question, "Who is God?" Ask your students to write or draw their answers. (Some may be: God is our Father, he is powerful, he is the creator of everything, etc.)

Look at the mural together and talk about what they wrote. As an introduction, tell them that today's story is about a special day in which God proved that He is the only true God.

DEVELOPMENT OF THE BIBLE STORY

Using recycled paper or newspaper, make two altars like the ones shown on the student worksheet. You can also draw some cuts of "meat" that represent the sacrifice.

Paste them in front of the room and tell the Bible story using the pictures as a reference. When you reach the part where God sends fire from heaven, place a illustration of fire flames (that you can make with red paper or cellophane paper) on the altar of Elijah.

It is very important that your students know that all of the stories that you present in the class are taken from the Bible, which is the Word of God. Encourage them to read the story in their own Bibles by way of review.

APPLICATION TO DAILY LIFE

Through Elijah's example, your students have learned the importance of recognizing God as the only supreme being in the universe. It is important that during this time, they identify that the God whom they praise is the one whom the prophet Elijah served.

Look for magazines, books, or illustrations that show natural demonstrations of God's power (for example, a lightning bolt, a waterfall, a volcano eruption, etc.). Show them to your students, noting that our powerful God controls nature and shows His power in various ways.

Provide them with white sheets of paper and colored pencils, so that they draw a picture of the way that they perceive the power of God in their life.

ACTIVITIES

God Shows That His is the Only God!

As you give your students their worksheets, briefly review what they have learned during the class. Ask them to fold the top of the worksheet down along the dotted line so they can see how God responded to Elijah's prayer.

Ask them, "Why do you think Baal did not answer the prayers of his prophets?" Listen to the answers and then comment that, although the prophets of Baal were many, they had no power because their god was fake. We know that God is the only true God. When he showed his power by sending fire from heaven to consume the sacrifice, the people decided to believe in him, they knelt down and said, "The Lord is God!"

James 5:16

Allow time for students to complete the Bible verse on their worksheet using the words on the hands.

When they have finished, repeat the text together and then have your students repeat it individually.

Review Questions

Divide the class into two groups and ask the following questions. The group that answers will earn five points for each correct answer. If a group doesn't know the answer, the other group will be able to answer and earn the 5 points. The team who manages to accumulate the most points will be the winner. If no one knows the answer to a question, briefly review that part of the lesson:

- ✘ Where did Elijah ask that all the prophets of Baal gather?
- ✘ What was the name of the wicked king who ruled the people of Israel?
- ✘ How long had there been no rain?
- ✘ What was the name of King Ahab's administrator?
- ✘ What challenge did the prophet Elijah give to the prophets of Baal?
- ✘ What happened when the prophets of Baal prayed?
- ✘ What happened when Elijah prayed?
- ✘ What was the reaction of the people when they saw God's response?
- ✘ Is the God of Elijah the same God we know?
- ✘ How does God show his power today?

MEMORIZATION

Help your students understand the memory verse better by searching in a Bible dictionary for the meaning of the words in this verse. For some of them, there will be some words that may be difficult to understand. It is important to clarify any doubts. They should have a better understanding of what they are learning. In this case define the words "prayer," "righteous" and "effective."

When you finish your explanation, use the worksheet to review the memory verse with your students.

CONCLUSION

Allow for a question and answer time as a final review. Invite your students to continue learning about the prophet Elijah in the next class, and guide them in prayer. It is very important that your students understand that prayer is a fundamental part of a Christian's life and it is also important that you set an example of what that looks like. Encourage them to bring prayer requests to the class so you can intercede for them together.

Thank God for hearing and answering the prayers of his people.

NOTES:

LESSON 47

GOD STRENGTHENS ELIJAH

GENERAL ASPECTS

Biblical Basis: 1 Kings 19

Memory Verse: "*The prayer of a righteous person is powerful and effective*" (James 5:16).

Lesson Objective: To teach students that they can seek God in times of need.

TEACHER'S PREPARATION

Elijah went through a period of great despair after he overcame the prophets of Baal. In Chapters 18 and 19 of 1 Kings we can see a dramatic change in attitude and in the behavior of the prophet, who went from courage to fear in an unexpected way.

After finishing with the prophets of Baal, Elijah became the target of Queen Jezebel. He fled from Israel, full of fear and despair. He went south and came to Beersheba, on the south-eastern border with Judea. Abandoning the city and firing his servant, Elijah turned his back on his prophetic ministry, thinking that he had already "had enough." In Judea, it was beyond the reach of Jezebel, but it was still in the land of the Lord.

God was not going to accept Elijah's fear because he had prepared more work for him (verses 15-18). The Lord was very patient with Elijah, though he fled. God did not condemn him for being frustrated and walking with his head down. On the contrary, he was aware of his needs and provided rest, food, direction and protection.

After sending an angel to strengthen him, God allowed Elijah to go even further into the desert, and even met him personally on Mount Horeb. It is very important that we realize how God, in spite of revealing himself through fire, wind and an earthquake, on this occasion spoke to Elijah in a gentle and sweet way (vv.11-13). The prophet was fearful, insecure, had left his ministry and his people behind. But God did not leave him alone and showed him that he was still with him.

ADAPTATION

Some children face different problems that create anxiety and fears, such as divorce, unemployed parents, and violence in schools, homes, and neighborhoods. All these factors affect the lives of the youngest. There are even situations that seem trivial to adults, but can be dangerous to the emotional stability of a young child.

Feeling down or depressed is not unusual. It is a normal part of the human experience. Poor nutrition, inadequate rest, and dramatic circumstances can trigger these reactions. This lesson will help children recognize that feelings of loneliness, sadness and discouragement are normal.

They will discover that even heroes like Elijah experienced such situations. Finally, the lesson teaches students what to do when they feel that way. Help them feel the assurance that God will help you when you're sad, lonely or discouraged.

LESSON DEVELOPMENT

Introduction

When Do You Feel Sad?

Before class, prepare a circle of paper with a sad face drawn on it.

In class, tell the children to form a circle and give them the sad face. The activity is to pass the paper off to each other until you, or some other student, says, "Stop." The child with the sad face in his hands should answer one of the following questions.

Repeat this until most of the children have participated in the game. If you want, you can add more questions:

- ✘ What kinds of situations make children feel sad, lonely, discouraged, or fearful?
- ✘ What can children do to overcome these feelings?
- ✘ Can people be discouraged like Elijah?
- ✘ What should people do when they feel discouraged?

Reflect with them by emphasizing that the prophet Elijah did very valuable things for God. Say, "In today's story, Elijah did not feel like a hero. This time, he felt sad, lonely and discouraged."

DEVELOPMENT OF THE BIBLE STORY

Using the student worksheets from the last class, briefly review what was taught in that lesson. Elijah had defeated the prophets of Baal and God had demonstrated his absolute sovereignty. The prophet was going through a time of anguish and despair. The queen was looking for him to kill him and he was very distressed.

Tell the story to your students as you read a few key verses from the Bible. If you have visual aids, they will be very helpful. If you don't have visual aids, try to make the story more real by being expressive with your voice.

Give your students the worksheets for today's lesson and rely on the pictures to better illustrate the development of the Bible story.

APPLICATION TO DAILY LIFE

Today, students learned that even men of faith like Elijah experience moments of fear and anguish. Help them identify themselves with this story and to understand that even in the midst of the most difficult problems, God is ready to help them.

Give each child a piece of paper, and ask them to write down what causes fear or distress. (Help those who can't write well.) Bring a container with a label that says, "God has everything under control." When all the children have written, tell them to leave their papers in the container as a way of putting their fears in the hands of God. Pray for them and invite them to trust the Lord when they feel sad.

Sadly, depression is a serious problem that is growing among our children. Many of them go through difficult situations in life that are beyond what they can bear. If you feel that some of your students are going through depression, pray for them and seek advice from your pastor or Sunday School Superintendent.

Your students should know that when they feel tired, hungry or sad, they can improve their mood by eating, resting, or talking to someone they trust. Sometimes it may be difficult for them to trust in God. Tell them to seek the Lord with faith in prayer, knowing that he will answer their requests.

Pray for all students in your class to feel encouraged throughout the week. Ask if there are prayer requests and pray for them.

Encouragement Cards

For this activity you will need drawing paper, markers or crayons, chalkboard, chalk, envelopes, scissors (optional), glue and decorations such as sequins, string, thread, or some trimmings. Before class, write on the chalkboard, "Cast all your anxiety on him because he cares for you" (1 Peter 5: 7).

Invite students to make small cards to encourage someone who is going through a difficult time. Give each one a piece of paper and ask them to fold it in half. They can draw a picture on the front or use the supplies you brought to decorate their card. Then help them write a sentence or phrase of encouragement on the inside of the card. They can be phrases like, "I care about you" or "With all my love."

Show the children the verse you wrote on the board. Explain that the words from the Bible are given as encouragement and strength to those who feel sad, lonely or discouraged. Let them write the verse on their cards. Encourage your students to give away the cards they made to someone who is going through a difficult time.

ACTIVITIES

Elijah Was Sad

Give each student the worksheet for today's lesson. Look in the CUTOUT section for the three additional pictures you will need to complete this activity. Have your students cut out the pictures and paste them in the corresponding boxes on their worksheets.

Review the Bible story while the students are working on this activity.

How Do You Feel?

Ask your students to color the little face that represents how they feel right now. Then read aloud the questions at the bottom of the page, and let them answer by making a mark in the corresponding column. If any of the answers are "yes" they should cut the colored strip on the left side to cover the question and then ask someone to give them advice as to what they should do.

MEMORIZATION

To review the memory verse, ask your students to form a circle. Stand in the middle and throw a soft ball to one of the children. The recipient should say the verse aloud and throw the ball back to you. Repeat the game until all of your students have participated.

CONCLUSION

Conclude the class by singing a chorus that talks about trusting in God, and encourage the children to take refuge in the Lord in times of need.

Encourage your students to tell others the story they learned about Elijah today.

Pray with the children before they are dismissed.

LESSON 48

GOD CONTINUES HIS WORK

GENERAL ASPECTS

Biblical Basis: 2 Kings 2:1-18

Memory Verse: "*The prayer of a righteous person is powerful and effective*" (James 5:16).

Lesson Objective: To help students understand that God is always with them and continues blessing them.

TEACHER'S PREPARATION

Elijah left this world in an unusual way. This fact is largely related to his ministry. The image of fire appeared on several occasions throughout his life: Mount Carmel (1 Kings 18:38), Mount Horeb (1 Kings 19:12), and Mount Samaria (2 Kings 1:10, 12). However, on this occasion the fire did not descend from heaven to destroy evil; it descended to take Elijah, who was the messenger of God to his people, into the presence of God. And when he left, people began to wonder who would be the new chosen one who would speak from God.

Very few people accept changes when they come into their lives. We get used to always doing the same thing, so we feel disturbed when there is a need to change something.

The change in Elisha's life when the prophet Elijah called him to be his successor changed the direction of the fate of this simple man of the field. Elisha accepted the Lord's challenge to serve him and, leaving everything behind, responded to his call.

Now his teacher and guide was about to be raptured by God. Elisha was facing a new and even greater change: being the voice of God on earth.

But this man of faith decided to trust in the Lord and to fulfill the mission that had been given to him.

ADAPTATION

Your students face many changes over the course of their life. They change teachers at school, their families move to other cities and meet new neighbors, their classmates change over the years, and so on. Others face deeper changes: the death of a family member, the divorce of their parents and new marriages. But despite these changes, God continues to bless his people with his presence.

As your students face these changes, help them know that God will always be with them and will continue to carry out the plans for all his children.

LESSON DEVELOPMENT

Introduction

Before starting the class, create a word search puzzle on the chalkboard with rows and columns of random letters, but with the word "change" hidden somewhere in the puzzle.

When the time comes for the Bible story, tell your students that there is a mysterious word that helps us introduce today's lesson. Give them time to discover the letters that form the word.

Talk about what the word "change" means (something different, unknown, new, etc.). Encourage a conversation in which children express what kinds of changes they have experienced in their lives and whether they liked them or not.

Tell them that this Biblical story tells of the great changes experienced by the prophet Elijah and his new friend Elisha.

DEVELOPMENT OF THE BIBLE STORY

Beforehand, cut a piece of cardboard in half. Write the name "Eljah" on one part and "Elisha" on the other.

Tell them, "In this story there are two people who have very similar names." Show the cards and point out the letters that are the same in both names, and then the letters that are different.

Narrate the Bible story and if possible use visual aids. If you wish, you can rely on the student workbook as a didactic resource. You can also draw pictures or ask someone to help you draw some of the most significant scenes in the story, and stick them on a poster board to make them more resilient.

Let your students ask all the questions they want and try to answer them as best you can. Encourage them to read and comment on their favorite part.

APPLICATION TO DAILY LIFE

Point out the great changes that took place in the lives of Elijah and Elisha. Emphasize that they were part of God's perfect plan.

Your students should recognize that, even though they often go through difficult periods of change and adjustment, they can trust that God will help them to not have fears, even in times of great need.

Write on the board the phrase, "Did you know?", and give them paper so they can write it as a title. At the bottom they should write down what they learned during the class, for example:

- ✘ Did you know that God helps me when I go to a new school?
- ✘ Did you know that God is with me when we move to another city?
- ✘ Did you know that God never changes and His power is eternal?

If they wish they can make drawings to decorate their pages.

ACTIVITIES

When Our Circumstances Change

Give your students the worksheet corresponding to this lesson, along with crayons or markers. Tell them, "Today we are talking about the changes we face in our lives. This activity will help us to remember what we have learned."

Allow some time for them to talk about what they think each of the pictures on the worksheet represents. Each picture represents a different situation that can occur when someone experiences change in their life. For example: moving to a new house, school or church; when a pastor or teacher leaves and a new one replaces them; the death of a loved one; the divorce of parents or a new marriage.

Instruct your students to follow the instructions and circle the illustration that represents a change they have had in their lives.

Elijah and Elisha

Have your students turn the worksheet over and give them scissors, glue or tape. They will also need the pictures from the CUTOUT section that go with this lesson. Read the instructions aloud.

Help them to cut along the solid black lines to avoid accidentally cutting too much.

Review the Story

Write the following questions on strips of paper and put them into a container. Have the children take a strip, read the question and answer it to earn a small prize (a bookmark, a treat, a pencil, etc.). You can add more questions depending on the number of students you have in your class:

- ✘ Who told Elisha that Elijah would be taken away by God?
- ✘ What did Elisha ask of Elijah before he went to heaven?
- ✘ What separated Elijah from Elisha?
- ✘ How did God take Elijah?
- ✘ What did Elisha do with the robe that fell from Elijah?
- ✘ What river did Elijah and Elisha cross?
- ✘ What can we do when changes occur in our lives?
- ✘ Who controls everything that happens in our life?
- ✘ Repeat the memory verse by heart (James 5:16).

MEMORIZATION

Because this is the last lesson of the unit, try to make arrangements with the Sunday School Superintendent or Pastor to have your class participate in worship by reciting the memory verse for the congregation. They can do it individually or together. This can be a time to recognize what your students have learned and a time to encouragement them.

CONCLUSION

Review what has been learned in the four lessons of the unit. Make a poster about the life of Elijah, and let your students write or draw on it the most important thing they learned about the ministry of this prophet.

Highlight the Biblical lessons you've taught and relate them to the daily lives of your students.

Pray for your students and ask God that the Word that has been sown in these tender hearts will bear fruit in abundance.

UNIT XI : THE GIFTS OF CHRISTMAS

Biblical Basis: Luke 1:26-38; 2:1-7, 8-20; Matthew 1:18-25; 2:1-12; John 3:16

Unit Theme Verse: *"For God so loved the world that he gave his one and only Son, that whoever believes in him shall not perish but have eternal life"* (John 3:16).

PURPOSE OF THIS UNIT

This unit will help your students:

- ✘ Appreciate the gift of God that is Jesus.
- ✘ Understand that Mary and Joseph gave themselves to be the earthly parents of Jesus.
- ✘ Experience the joy of giving when they follow the example of the shepherds and wise men.
- ✘ Learn that the best gifts are not material things.
- ✘ Know that Christmas is a time to celebrate the birth of Jesus.
- ✘ Understand that these lessons will encourage you to tell others the good news of the birth of Jesus.
- ✘ Obey and worship Jesus, the Son of God.

UNIT LESSONS

Lesson 49: Mary and Joseph's Gifts

Lesson 50: God's Gift

Lesson 51: The Shepherds' Gifts

Lesson 52: The Gifts of the Magi

WHY WE NEED TO TEACH THIS UNIT

Christmas is the favorite time of year for most children. They have a great admiration for this time of year. It is very easy for them to get lost or confused among secular celebrations, so they need a clear teaching of what Christmas really means.

They must know that God is the supreme example of one who gives when He gave us His only Son, Jesus Christ. Take time to read stories straight from the Bible. Each lesson contains a creative monologue of a character in the story. These will help the children to imagine themselves in the events that occurred during the birth of Jesus.

Students will be moved by the angel, the fear and admiration of a shepherd, and the stillness of a wise man. These characters will help children learn about the joy of giving. They will also learn that the greatest joy of Christmas is to give their love to Jesus and to people.

Pass on to each student's heart that Christmas should be the most important celebration of the year. We celebrate the best gift ever given: God gave us His Son Jesus Christ!

Encourage them to give an important gift to Jesus: their own life. Take advantage of these lessons so that your students surrender their lives to the Lord.

LESSON 49

MARY AND JOSEPH'S GIFTS

GENERAL ASPECTS

Biblical Basis: Luke 1:26-38; Matthew 1:18-25

Memory Verse: *"For God so loved the world that he gave his one and only Son, that whoever believes in him shall not perish but have eternal life"* (John 3:16).

Lesson Objective: That students will learn that the best gifts are not material things.

TEACHER'S PREPARATION

In Jewish tradition, marriage ceremonies lasted a whole year. The fiancée lived with her friends or family until the time of the wedding. These wedding engagements were very serious. All the belongings of the bride were given to the future husband.

To break with that commitment, there must be a separation. If the future wife commits adultery, it signifies her dishonor, and she must die by being stoned. In Luke 1:26-38, we see that the angel Gabriel appeared before Mary in Galilee, a young virgin engaged to Joseph, and told her that she would give birth to a son. Imagine the conflict she faced! What would Joseph do? What would the town people say? How could this happen?

Despite what this would cost her, Mary accepted the message kindly and decided to obey the will of God. She was to name the baby, Jesus. Many named their sons Joshua, or Jeshua, in the hope that it would be the expected Messiah or a leader of the Israelite people. But on this occasion, God demanded that the child be called Jesus because he would be the Redeemer, the long-awaited Messiah announced by the prophecies.

After hearing this news, Mary responded in obedience to the Lord, "I am the servant of the Lord. May it happen just as you have told me" (verse 38). She gave herself completely to the plans of God, not caring what the consequences might entail.

Matthew 1:18-25 refers to the moment when Joseph learned of the pregnancy of his promised wife, and instead of dishonoring or stoning Mary, he decided to separate from her in secret because he loved her and did not want to expose her to a lifetime of ridicule.

In the hour of Joseph's desperation, an angel appeared to him in a dream and told him that Mary was waiting for the Son of God to save the people from their sins. Joseph believed and did everything as God had told him to do through the angel.

This fulfilled the prophecy of the prophet Isaiah, who had said, "Behold, the virgin shall conceive and bear a son, and shall call his name Emmanuel" (7:14), which means "God with us." The message that the angel gave to Mary and Joseph was very similar. He told them that the child would be the Son of God and that they would call him Jesus. They accepted and surrendered to be the earthly parents of Jesus.

ADAPTATION

Our culture is overwhelmingly materialistic in all aspects. Sadly, Christmas is one of the most materialistic times of the year. Questions like: "What gift do you want for Christmas?" or "What did you get for Christmas?" bombard children.

Maybe some of your students feel sad about not being able to buy gifts or not receiving as many as they would like. Children need a new perspective on this. We must help them know that the best gifts cannot be bought, but can only be given. The best gift their parents or anyone else can give them is love, not a toy. As a result, children will learn to give love to God, their parents and others.

LESSON DEVELOPMENT

Introduction

Briefly introduce this unit, emphasizing that during these next four lessons, we will study Christmas gifts and that it is important that they attend faithfully. Write the following question on the chalkboard: "How can we know that our parents love and care for us?"

(The children will give answers like: they buy us clothes and food, they play with us, they help us with our school homework, they read us stories, they take us to the doctor when we are sick, they give us a home and a place to sleep, etc.)

Show a box wrapped as a gift. Say, "This box reminds us that our parents give us many gifts."

"Some of us receive them for vacations or at Christmas. Other gifts can be love, care, help and comfort. Today's Bible story is about two very special parents. Listen and see what gifts they gave their baby.

DEVELOPMENT OF THE BIBLE STORY

Tell your students the story of Mary and Joseph, and how they prepared to receive their new son. You can have children act out the story while you're telling it. Remind them that God chose Mary and Joseph as the earthly parents of Jesus because they responded with maturity, integrity, and faithfulness. They would provide a good home for His Son. Emphasize the love and care with which Mary and Joseph gave baby Jesus.

Invite a couple from your church who have just become parents or have a baby and let your group know how they care for and protect their little child. Children can ask questions and participate with them.

Encourage your students to think about what they can do for their parents this Christmas. Tell them, "Like Mary and Joseph, most parents give love and care for their children. What can we do to show love to our parents and those who take care of us?"

If they cannot think of anything, give them some suggestions. Those could be: cleaning your room, taking out the trash, picking up your toys, etc. Instruct the children to give these "gifts of love" to their parents during Christmas and all year round.

APPLICATION TO DAILY LIFE

Relate the Biblical story to the daily life of your students. Remind them that the most important gifts are not material gifts, but to express our love and affection to the people who love us.

Tell the children that just as Joseph took loving care of Jesus, God loves and cares for us and wants us to love him in the same way.

Ask, "What do you think is the greatest test of God's love for us?" The answer is that he sent his only Son Jesus into this world to be the promised Messiah, our Savior.

God also asks that we love our neighbor. Ask children to tell you who their neighbors are. Emphasize the importance of loving everyone equally. Remember, the main idea of this lesson is for children to learn that Christmas is not just a time for material gifts, but to celebrate with joy the birth of Jesus and the love of God for all of us.

Reflect on this lesson with your students and invite them to make a commitment to be more loving to their parents and to God. Pray with them and thank God for their love and care.

ACTIVITIES

Stand Up, Angel!

Give your students the worksheet, scissors and glue. Help them cut out the figure of the angel and decorate it however they'd like to. Glue the side of the dress that is marked to the back edge of the other side of the dress (making a cylinder), so that the angel can stand up.

While working on the angel, review the Bible story with your students.

Christmas Cards

Prepare these materials in advance. You will need white cards or paper, envelopes, stamps, pictures, Christmas stickers, glue, scissors, colored paper, glitter, markers and colors.

Give your students paper or pre-cut cardstock the size of a greeting card. Ask your students to make a Christmas card for their parents, grandparents or whoever they want.

MEMORIZATION

Cut out several large circles and decorate them to look like Christmas ornaments. Write the memory verse on the ornaments, dividing it into short phrases. Hang the ornaments in the front of the classroom and read it aloud to your students. Then mix the ornaments up and allow time for your students to put them in the correct order. Say the verse out loud together. Repeat the exercise several times.

CONCLUSION

Sing a song before saying goodbye and briefly review the lesson. Invite the children to come again next week. Encourage them to bring a friend so they can share with them the good news of Christmas.

Pray for the requests of your students and keep in touch with them during the week.

NOTES:

LESSON 50

GOD'S GIFT

GENERAL ASPECTS

Biblical Basis: Luke 2:1-7; John 3:16

Memory Verse: *"For God so loved the world that he gave his one and only Son, that whoever believes in him shall not perish but have eternal life"* (John 3:16).

Lesson Objective: To help students learn that Christmas is a celebration of Jesus' birth.

TEACHER'S PREPARATION

Emperor Caesar Augustus ordered a census of the entire Roman empire. Everyone was ordered to go to the city of their birth, where they were to register and pay their taxes. Joseph and Mary were descendants of King David. For this reason Joseph was to return to Bethlehem. It was a three days' journey from Nazareth. While they were in Bethlehem, the time came for the birth of Jesus. And this was fulfilled by the prophet Micah (Micah 5: 2).

Mary and Joseph looked for a place to stay but all the inns were full. However, some inns at that time had stables to guard the travelers' animals. These were sometimes cold and dark, but it was there that God showed His immense mercy to mankind by the birth of His Son Jesus. Mary wrapped the baby in diapers and laid him in a manger; there lay God's greatest gift for all, his Son Jesus!

John 3:16 is considered the golden verse of the Bible and the heart of the gospel. It shows the gift God gave in all its splendor. He gave us his Son to give us eternal life!

ADAPTATION

It is likely that your students do not understand that Christmas is the celebration of Jesus' birth. This date should be the most important date for children, but sometimes, for wrong reasons, this is not the case. Receiving gifts and social celebrations become a priority for people.

Christmas should be the most important celebration of the year. We celebrate the best gift ever given. God gave His Son! Help your students discover in Jesus the best gift of all.

LESSON DEVELOPMENT

Introduction

Invite your students to express what they like most about Christmas. Some will give answers about receiving toys or clothes, seeing their family or doing something special with their parents. Let them freely express their answers. You will quickly learn their perception of Christmas.

Write on the chalkboard, "What does your family do to celebrate Christmas?" Invite them to tell about the religious celebrations they have experienced in their family, such as going to church or reading the story of Jesus' birth in the Bible. Ask them how they imagine Christmas. After hearing the answers, tell them that God sent His Son as the most precious gift to be our Savior, and that Christians celebrate the birth of Jesus at Christmas.

DEVELOPMENT OF THE BIBLE STORY

Tell your students the context of the story. Tell them about the journey that Joseph and Mary made to get to Bethlehem, and the problems they faced in order to get a place to stay. It is important that they understand that the birth of Jesus occurred in the midst of special and unexpected circumstances. He received no honors or attention as the king of the earth, but on the contrary, He came to the world in a humble way to show he was a servant.

To visualize the history of this day, you can use some illustrative teaching material if you have it. If not, make it yourself or buy some pictures used in traditional Christmas packets (there are some inexpensive ones) to represent the characters in the story (Mary, Joseph and the angel). Take advantage of all the resources that you can find.

If you wish, you can invite a young man from the congregation to help you tell the Biblical story disguised as Joseph. Have him tell the class his experience during the journey and the birth of Jesus. Children can actively participate by asking questions.

APPLICATION TO DAILY LIFE

After hearing the Bible story, it is almost certain that your students will have changed their way of thinking about Christmas. Reinforce this idea in their minds and hearts, telling them that the birth of Jesus is the beginning of God's plan to save mankind from their sins. That plan includes them. God sent His only Son, Jesus Christ, as a gift of love, and that's the reason we celebrate Christmas.

ACTIVITIES

Nativity Scene

Give your students the worksheet for this lesson, scissors, and glue or tape.

Begin by having your students cut out the stable and the pictures at the bottom of the worksheet along the solid black lines. Then fold along the dotted lines under the stable; starting at the bottom, fold forward, then backward and repeat. This should create folds or channels where your students can glue or tape into place the figures of Mary, Joseph, Jesus and the animals. (If you wish, you can attach cardboard to the back of the stable to make it sturdier.)

When they have finished, have them practice telling a friend in the class the story of Christmas. Encourage them to take their Nativity Scenes home and share the story with their friends and family.

Christmas Wreath

For this activity you will need green construction paper or other heavy duty green paper, glue, scissors, pencils and a red ribbon.

Give each of your students a piece of green paper and a pencil, and have them trace around one of their open hands.

When they are finished, help each of them cut out their hand, and if they want they can decorate them. Have them put their name in the center of their hand.

Before class, cut out a large paper ring, large enough to fit all your students' cut out hands on it. When all the students hands are cut out, glue them onto the ring at the base of the hand, forming a wreath. It is important to make sure that all the hands are placed close together so that the wreath looks better.

To finish, decorate the Christmas wreath with a red ribbon at the top, and put it in your classroom where everyone can see it.

What Can I Give?

Talk to your students about the gift of giving. Say, "It's fun to give and receive gifts. How do you feel when you give a gift to someone?" (Let your students comment.) "Is it not true that when we give someone a gift, it is fun to see their face when they receive it and open it? We have talked about giving gifts to others in the last two lessons."

"What has been the best gift that was ever given?" (When God gave us His Son, Jesus.) "That is why we celebrate Christmas."

MEMORIZATION

Have your students look in their Bibles for the memory verse John 3:16: *"For God so loved the world that he gave his one and only Son, that whoever believes in him shall not perish but have eternal life."*

First read it together and then read it out loud. Ask the children the following questions (they should answer keeping their Bibles closed):

- ✘ Who did God love? (The World.)
- ✘ According to the memory verse, who did God give? (His one and only son)
- ✘ Why did God send His Son? (Because He loves us.)
- ✘ What happens to those who believe in the Son of God? (They will have everlasting life.)
- ✘ What is the name of God's Son? (Jesus.)

CONCLUSION

Each Sunday, the celebration of Christmas is closer, and it is a good time to prepare the hearts of your students to give others the gift of love that God gave through his Son Jesus. Encourage your students to invite their friends to Sunday school.

Do not forget to ask if there are prayer requests and to include them as you pray for the class. Children are comforted to know that you are interested in their problems. Encourage them to attend the next class to continue discovering the Gifts of Christmas.

LESSON 51

THE SHEPHERDS' GIFTS

GENERAL ASPECTS

Biblical Basis: Luke 2:8-20

Memory Verse: *"For God so loved the world that he gave his one and only Son, that whoever believes in him shall not perish but have eternal life"* (John 3:16).

Lesson Objective: To help students share with others the good news of Jesus' birth.

TEACHER'S PREPARATION

The Gospel of Luke is the only gospel that tells us about the angel's visit to the shepherds during the night as they tended their sheep near Bethlehem, in a small and unknown city. But Bethlehem was a city rich in history. And Rachel, the wife of Jacob, was buried there when the city was called Ephrath.

Bethlehem was the home of Naomi, Ruth, and Boaz. It was there that the prophet Samuel met David, the future king of Israel. Micah prophesied that the Messiah himself would be born in Bethlehem. The angel's announcement was very clear when he told them who Jesus was. He called him "Savior" and "Christ the Lord" (Luke 2:11).

Perhaps the shepherds interpreted this as if he was to become a military or political savior that would lead the people of Israel to form a great nation. His birth was good news for all (v.10), not just for the more powerful Jews. The birth of Jesus was good news even for the most humble person on earth.

The announcement that the angels made to the shepherds is still valid today. Year after year we celebrate the glorious truth that Jesus, the Son of God, came to this world to save us from our sins.

ADAPTATION

Your students know that they are among the youngest students in their elementary school. They came from "kindergarten" or "preschool" where they were the eldest, and now they have to adjust to their new condition of being the smallest of the school. They are going through a transition from leaving the security of their homes, where perhaps they are the center of attention, to confront a large and unknown place where they feel unprotected.

It is natural for students to suffer under these conditions. Many cannot wait to be bigger to enjoy the privileges that "older children" enjoy. Children of this age will identify with the story of the shepherds.

The shepherds were low class people, humble, and often poor. Even so, God considered them important and thus they were to be the first to know the good news of Jesus' birth.

Encourage your students to experience the hope, joy, and reverence that those shepherds felt when they heard the angel's announcement. God cares for everyone, including those who are very humble.

The shepherds did not have expensive gifts to bring to Jesus. All they had to offer was their worship. Like them, children often have little to give. Help them see that God values the worship they give Him.

Just as the shepherds gave the good news, they can also tell others about the birth of Jesus. Young children do not know what it means to be an evangelist or a preacher, yet they know they can tell others what they have learned. Even at an early age they can help spread the gospel.

LESSON DEVELOPMENT

Introduction

Ask your students how they would feel if their best friend did not share their new toys with them. You will hear answers such as "sad," "hurt," "I would feel my friend is selfish," etc. Also, ask them how they would feel if someone knew something important and did not tell them. Say, "In today's story, you will learn about some people who heard a very important message, and now, a very special guest will be in charge of giving that great message to you."

DEVELOPMENT OF THE BIBLE STORY

Invite ahead of time a young man or adult in your congregation to represent a shepherd. You can also use a puppet to tell the Bible story. This way the children will listen to the story more realistically and identify with the guest character. Whichever option you choose, you must deliver the Bible study passage in time to the special guest and explain what the emphasis is on today's story.

Have the children form a semicircle and present the guest (if using a puppet take the necessary precautions to set up a simple stage). Tell them that someone who has a very important story to share with them is visiting today.

Allow time for the guest, and when they are done, allow your students time to ask questions and interact with the guest.

APPLICATION TO DAILY LIFE

After the guest has said goodbye, ask the children what they liked most about the visit.

When you have listened to all the answers, talk again with your group about the enthusiasm of the shepherd as he recounted the news the angel had given him. He was very happy and wanted to announce the good news to everyone. Like the shepherds, we also know the good news of salvation, and we must tell others.

Encourage your students to tell their families and friends the news that Jesus, the Son of God, was born in Bethlehem to be the Savior of all who would receive him.

ACTIVITIES

The Shepherd's Cube

You will need the worksheet for this lesson, as well as scissors and glue.

Help the children cut out the shape along the solid black lines, taking care not to cut the tabs that will be used to put the cube together. When you have finished cutting, fold the shape along the dotted lines to form a box. Use one of the cubes as an example and point to the sequence of events that make up today's Bible story. Using the drawings on the cube, review the lesson with your students and ask them to put a number in each square according to the order in which the story took place.

Turn the page over and read the memory verse (John 3:16). Then fold the tabs at the ends and glue them into the appropriate places to assemble the cube.

Wait until the glue is dry before letting the children handle the cubes. It is likely that if there are very young children in your group, they will need additional help to complete this activity. These cubes can serve as a tool to help your students tell their friends the story of how the shepherds went to Bethlehem in search of the baby Jesus to worship him.

The Angels and Shepherds

Give each student a white sheet of paper, crayons, and markers.

Have them draw the scene in which the angels announce to the shepherds the birth of Jesus. When they are finished, you can put the pictures around the room and invite their parents and the members of the congregation to visit your exhibit. Let the children be in charge of telling what happened on this special visit that the shepherds received.

MEMORIZATION

Have your students sit in a circle and place yourself in the center. Throw them a light ball. The child who receives it should stand and say the verse by heart (John 3:16). Repeat this exercise so all of your students participate. Help any students who are struggling with memorization.

CONCLUSION

To conclude, pray, thanking God for the Christmas holiday and what it represents. Praise him for sending Jesus as a gift of love to us and ask him to help each of the students tell others the story of Christmas.

Encourage your students to use the shepherds' story to tell others that Jesus came to earth as a baby to save the world from their sins.

NOTES:

LESSON 52

THE GIFTS OF THE MAGI

GENERAL ASPECTS

Biblical Basis: Matthew 2:1-12

Memory Verse: *"For God so loved the world that he gave his one and only Son, that whoever believes in him shall not perish but have eternal life"* (John 3:16).

Lesson Objective: To encourage students to worship and obey Jesus.

TEACHER'S PREPARATION

The story of the visit of the Magi to see Jesus is one of the most exciting parts of the Christmas story. It tells us about the long journey they took to see the newborn king. The Bible does not tell us how many magi visited Jesus, or what their names were. Tradition says there were three, because of the number of gifts they offered to the Lord. However, they could have been more than three.

But the Bible gives us some clear facts. The magi came from the east to Jerusalem, and went to King Herod to ask, "Where is the king of the Jews born? For his star we have seen in the east, and we come to worship him" (Matthew 2: 2).

The King Herod of this passage should not be confused with the other kings of the same name mentioned in the Bible. This king was not a Jew, but a cruel and very jealous man. And he did not want another king to take his place.

Herod did not know of any unborn baby being "the king of the Jews." "And when he had called all the chief priests and the scribes of the people, he asked them where the Christ should be born" (verse 4).

When they gave him the answer, they said to him, "In Bethlehem of Judea; For thus it is written by the prophet" (verse 5). The prophet to whom this passage refers is Micah (Micah 5: 2).

Immediately, "Herod secretly called the wise men." He wanted to know the exact time the star had appeared, in order to calculate the age of the child. So he sent them to Bethlehem to look for the baby, and told them that when they found him, they should let him know so that he could worship him.

When the magi left the palace of the King, they followed the star to Bethlehem, where Jesus was with his mother, Mary. Contrary to popular belief, he was not in the stable. Experts have established that Jesus was already one or two years old when the magi found him. This explains why afterwards Herod had all the children under two years of age living in Bethlehem killed.

When the magi found Jesus, they knelt before him and worshiped him, offering him very expensive gifts: gold, frankincense, and myrrh. These gifts symbolized what Jesus had come to do on this earth. Gold was a gift to kings. Jesus was a king. Frankincense was the gift to priests. Christ came to be our High Priest so that we could come into the presence of God without the help of an earthly priest. Myrrh was a gift to the one who was going to die. Jesus came to die for our sins.

The magi were warned by a vision in dreams that they should not return to Herod, because he wanted to kill the child. He was afraid that Jesus would take his place on the throne. So for that reason, the magi returned to their land in the east another way.

Just as these material gifts were important for their value and symbolism, the gifts of worship and obedience of these magi showed that the new Messiah had come for all, not only for the Jews. From the humble shepherds to the wise magi, all came to worship him. Even in our time, Christ reaches out to people of all social levels. He can reach everyone!

ADAPTATION

All children are fascinated with gifts, so for them, Christmas is a very important time. Children are thrilled to receive at least one present. Talk to them about their Christmas traditions.

It is sad to see that in our materialistic age, the gifts can tarnish the celebration of the birth of Jesus. Children sometimes worry a lot about what they are going to receive, forgetting how this tradition began.

The interests of the children as to what to receive for Christmas contrasts with what the magi decided to give to Jesus. They made a long journey to offer the King their gifts of worship and obedience, along with the gifts of gold, frankincense and myrrh. Help your students follow the example of the magi and give Jesus their full worship and obedience.

LESSON DEVELOPMENT

Introduction

Ask the children how they can show others that they are special to them. Answers may be "giving them a small gift," "lending them my toys," "being friendly," etc. Tell them, "Magi from the east came to see Jesus. They wanted to show him that he was a very special baby. Let's see what the magi did."

DEVELOPMENT OF THE BIBLE STORY

Prepare in advance three boxes (gifts) that represent the gifts of the magi, and place them in the front of the room. Write the words "gold," "incense" and "myrrh" on three different cards and place them inside each box.

Ask your students to try to guess the contents of the gifts that the magi brought to Jesus. As a response, relate the Bible story taking care not to leave out any details. When you mention the gifts that each magi brought to Jesus, open each of the boxes and let the children read the contents of the card.

Tell them that these gifts were offered to very important people, and symbolized the mission that Jesus had come to fulfill on earth. But material gifts were not the most important thing the wise men offered. Rather, it was their humility, obedience and praise which they put at the feet of the Messiah.

The magi were sensitive to the voice of God and returned to their land another way, giving thanks for having met the Savior of the world.

APPLICATION TO DAILY LIFE

Children learned today about the gifts of the magi, not only the material gifts, but also those that came from the bottom of their hearts. Explain that obedience and worship cannot be bought, but is born out of the depths of our feelings, and God desires that we give them to Him alone. Encourage them to put at Jesus' feet the best they have ... their little hearts willing to praise and obey Him.

ACTIVITIES

The Gifts of the Magi

Give your students the worksheet, glue and scissors. They will also need the gifts of the magi from the CUTOUT Section at the back of the student book. Have them cut out the gifts and glue them in the hands of the magi who are offering the gifts to baby Jesus.

Read the Bible verse on the worksheet and review briefly what you learned in the lesson today.

What Gifts Can We Give To Jesus?

Remind your students that we can all give gifts of praise and obedience to King Jesus. Have them turn their worksheets over and ask them the following question: "What gifts can we give Jesus?"

Help your students identify the different ways in which we can praise and obey God during this coming week. Provide colored pencils or crayons for your students and give them enough time to draw inside the gift boxes ways in which they can offer a present of obedience and praise to Jesus.

If some wish, they can tell the rest of the class what they decided to give Jesus. Read together the verse at the bottom of the worksheet (Acts 20:35).

The Star Inside an Apple

Cut an apple in half and show your students the star that forms in the middle of the apple. Tell them that some people think that the star in the middle of the apple is a reminder of the star that guided the Magi to where Jesus was. We are glad that God has sent that special star. It is a sign that Jesus is not only the King of the Jews, but also of us. The Magi who came from the East were the first non-Jewish people to worship Jesus. If you have enough apples, give them to the children as a small snack.

MEMORIZATION

If you can, have your students recite their memory verse for the whole congregation.

Congratulate them on their enthusiasm for learning the Word of God.

CONCLUSION

Give thanks to God for the gift of His Son, Jesus. As you pray, give thanks for Mary, Joseph, the shepherds and the Magi who came to visit the Messiah. Encourage your students to put into practice the lessons they have learned during this unit and to honor Jesus throughout their lives.

THE IMPORTANCE OF STUDENTS ADVANCING IN SUNDAY SCHOOL

Dear Leader and Sunday School Teacher;

As in elementary school, children in our church Sunday Schools should be able to be promoted to a higher level of Sunday School. As a classroom teacher, it is very important that you be prepared to promote the students at the end of the church year or, at the end of the school year - whichever is easiest. To accomplish this, talk to the Sunday School Superintendent of your church or your pastor.

You can prepare in advance a "ceremony" and give a certificate to each child passing to the next class. The ceremony can be performed in the sanctuary for all the congregation to participate in. Invite parents and relatives of the children. This will be a good time for them to get to know and attend the rest of the service and hear the Word of God.

It is important to have teachers of the classes that the children are graduating from and entering into as Special participants in the ceremony. It will be a special time for them to say goodbye to their present teacher with a hug, and for the teacher of the next class to welcome them to their new class with a hug. At the ceremony, you can present a card decorated with photos of the children that have been taken during the year. It can include some memories of the child's participation while he was in class, Special prayers they said, the date in which they gave their testimony, questions that they asked, and moments of joy experienced in the class. Prepare the child in advance, so they are not surprised in front of the entire congregation.

Talk to the Sunday School Superintendent so that at the ceremony the new Sunday School book for the following year can be given to the student(s.)You can encourage the families of the church to give a book to each child (as if they were the godparents), especially the children whose parents do not attend church or are at an economic disadvantage. In every congregation there are adults whose children are already adults who would gladly participate by giving a book to a child who attends Sunday School.

It is understandable if, because of a lack of teachers, it is not possible to have classes for every age group. This however is a good reason to invite and bring more children to church, and also to prepare and train new teachers. In every congregation there are always teenagers that are eager to learn how to teach a class. Do not miss this opportunity!

We wish you the richest blessings in the challenges that the ministry of education presents to you and your congregation.

In Christ and His Ministry,

Discipleship Ministries

Sunday School / Christian Education Materials for Children

Discipleship Ministries of the Mesoamerica Region presents its complete collection of books on Sunday School/Christian education. They were designed for teachers of children and for students from 4 to 11 years of age. Children will learn the lessons of the Bible according to their age. At the end of their elementary school years, they will have gone through the challenging biblical stories as well as various appropriate themes for each stage of their childhood and pre-teenage years. This material was designed as different steps to achieve a holy life. It contains clear and possible goals. The teacher's book will help equip those who have the beautiful task of leading children to connect with the message that will change their lives forever.

By promoting the child to the next year of class - according to his age - he will have studied only once each of the books. When he is 12 years old - if he started with the first book - he will have studied the eight books of this valuable collection.

The books were designed to be used in Sunday School, Children's Club, Discipleship, and Schools in general.

This series aims to:

- Challenge children to learn the Word of God.
- Allow them to grow in their Christian experience as children of God.
- Help them grow in their faith.
- Guide them to accept Jesus as their Savior and Lord.
- Help them to become part of the faith community - the church.

The following will help you identify the appropriate book according to the age of the students:

- Preschoolers - 4 and 5 years old (Year / Book 1 and 2).
- Elementary - 6 to 8 years old (Year / Book 1, 2 and 3).
- Words of Life (pre-adolescents) - 9 to 11 years old (Year / Book 1, 2 and 3).

www.ingramcontent.com/pod-product-compliance
Lightning Source LLC
Chambersburg PA
CBHW081541040426
42448CB00015B/3181
9781635800746